POST-CORONA
ECONOMY:
A REVIEW AND RESURRECTION

POST-CORONA ECONOMY:
A REVIEW AND RESURRECTION

A Way of Self-Reliance with a "0" Balance Society in Health, Literacy & Employment

SHYAMAL CHAKRABORTY

PARTRIDGE

Copyright © 2021 by Shyamal Chakraborty.

ISBN:	Hardcover	978-1-5437-0749-6
	Softcover	978-1-5437-0748-9
	eBook	978-1-5437-0750-2

All rights reserved. No part of this book may be used or reproduced by any means, graphic, electronic, or mechanical, including photocopying, recording, taping or by any information storage retrieval system without the written permission of the author except in the case of brief quotations embodied in critical articles and reviews.

Because of the dynamic nature of the Internet, any web addresses or links contained in this book may have changed since publication and may no longer be valid. The views expressed in this work are solely those of the author and do not necessarily reflect the views of the publisher, and the publisher hereby disclaims any responsibility for them.

Cover by: Sri Sayar Chakraborty

Print information available on the last page.

To order additional copies of this book, contact
Partridge India
000 800 919 0634 (Call Free)
+91 000 80091 90634 (Outside India)
orders.india@partridgepublishing.com

www.partridgepublishing.com/india

DEDICATION

On the auspicious day of offerings of water, in memory of my parents, who directed my life, saying, 'When and wherever you work, remember that it is in some way a part of your service to your motherland. Then be punctual, committed, and honest, with dedication to give your best to the assigned work,' I am dedicating my book to all those workers who died and the millions of workers eagerly waiting to serve the nations.

Shyamal Chakraborty
17 September 2020
Mahalaya

CONTENTS

Foreword ix
Acknowledgements xi
A Synopsis of the Book xiii

Chapter 1   Elementary..1
Chapter 2   Covid-19 Pre-, Present, Post- (PPP) 15
Chapter 3   Let Me Live 41
Chapter 4   A Healthy Nation....................................55
Chapter 5   A Smart Nation..75
Chapter 6   Every Man Has His Work 93
Chapter 7   Save, Spread, And Save...................... 111
Chapter 8   Self-Reliance 145
Chapter 9   Workers' Rest House 'Jatiya
                Karmi Awas' 157
Chapter 10 We Are All United 169

References... 181

FOREWORD

Today, the seventeenth day of September 2020, an auspicious day of the year in India, a dream project is placed in front of you and all my friends in India and abroad.

On such an auspicious day like Mahalaya, we fear an offering of water called *Tarpana* to our ancestors and gods together in fear of the corona pandemic. A small devastating virus has abruptly changed our lives. All living parameters, like schools, colleges, business establishments, etc. are either closed, broken off, or forced to suspend operations. In such crucial conditions, we have to revive our distressed economy and save the country. At a time of such destruction of the world economy, we hope to run beforehand to rebuild the socio-economic structure of the nation in a more concrete, progressive, and protective manner. This book deals with the same possibilities of a lasting and practical solution to challenge the situation, in line with economic practices, like increasing demand, supply, production, and consumption, and social concern. We, the nations, deserve a peaceful, happy, smart society with zero negativities in our social, financial, and cultural life. An attempt has been made here in this book to unveil the possibilities of building up a smart, self-dependent, healthy nation with a zero balance in national education, health, and employment.

There may be differences in the views, arguments, and opinions of our friends. It is obvious and expected in all times, but I hope no one will ultimately refuse to believe that the scarcity of money in hand is the bone of contention of all social and family incidents and conflicts in order. The peace and bonding amongst family members will also break down for money. When every workable hand has a job, when every citizen gets proper education and health support starting from childhood, there is no doubt that the civil and political crisis will be diminished.

The book is in simple English for everyone and without critical mathematics and equations that might bore readers. The data in this book was collected from national and international organisations' published open data and reports. I shall be blessed if this book can yield some positive results in national and social economics.

S. Chakraborty
17 September 2020
Odisha

ACKNOWLEDGEMENTS

It is my great pleasure to convey my heartfelt gratitude to all those who directly and indirectly enriched my feelings and inspired me to write this book.

First, I acknowledge my gratitude for the help of national and international Public and Private organisations for their information, data etc. published in open forum of websites. Without help of global data, information and reports on health, nature, education, economy, human society etc., published in open forum of websites, this work was impossible.

The pathos, agonies, and millions of deaths of the common masses due to the corona pandemic, and the obligatory suspension and closure of economic lifelines in countries have disrupted human lives. The common workers especially, at every level of human society, have been suffering miserably during the COVID-19 pandemic. I pay my homage and gratitude to the millions of deceased souls of workers; the great COVID warriors, like doctors, nurses, and health workers; the millions of jobless people of our nations; and the living gods and goddesses in the hospitals, who directly and indirectly pained, influenced, and compelled me to come forward with my dream project, for the benefit of the common masses of the world.

I am indebted to my wife, who took the pain of lots of negligence from my side yet who tirelessly supported me. I also wish to convey my gratitude to all my family members and relatives and my son, Sriman Sayar Chakraborty, who provided me enormous support with his art and illustrations to complete my book. I do also acknowledge and express my gratitude for all my friends, colleagues, and others who directly and indirectly helped me develop my feelings and experiences through their positive association.

I would like to show my gratitude to the publication house and the entire team for their great effort to bring the book to life.

It is not a book only; it is a dream of my life that I would like to spread, like a pandemic of civilisation, to every human heart and mind of the global society, with a hope to raise consciousness for a better, smarter, more literate, healthier, and more self-dependent active world society.

A SYNOPSIS OF THE BOOK

The ongoing pandemic, COVID-19, is in its juvenile phase. It has already spread over virtually all nations of the globe. To get rid of the deadly coronavirus, preventive and healing medicine is being invented by scientists throughout the world. It may arrive one day and read over the pandemic—only the history of epidemics and pandemics from the ancient period has shown that it will not vanish forever. It will ultimately remain like a dormant volcano and may break out from time to time low and high. It will live longer within living bodies, like animal and human bodies, as a parasite in latent form.

To get permanent and long-lasting relief from all viruses and other prolonged morbidities with malnutrition of children and mothers, Child wasting, cardiovascular disease, neonatal & liver, etc., the better hygienic and economic solution is to *cure a soul, not the sickness*. The disease comes in a thousand variants, but a healthy body can overcome it. A frail and unhealthy body becomes an abode of disease. A stable resurrection in socio-economic structure is all-important.

There should be a single digitalised, centrally held and monitored *national citizen life card* with an individual ID number, to be issued at the time of release of a baby for postbirth medication, vaccinations, healthcare, and education, in government or private health centres, schools, and service programmes. The same card should be treated as a voter identification card and used for income tax, economic activities, and everything else, till death. The card, being a digitally controlled total citizen profile, will be at people's fingertips and will reduce the various enumeration expenditures.

The health drive should start from the day of a baby's birth. The wellness of every child should be monitored under a common health mission for up to fifteen years or more. The girl child will be given particular priority in nutrition, education, and health, because she is the creator of the human universe.

In the mission to provide healthcare for all and to get rid of malnutrition, child death, high morbidity rates, etc., every school, from pre-nursery to the higher secondary level, should have a permanent full-time doctor and nurse with a medical facility and chamber for treatment, training, and health education, to build up a healthy nation.

A zero-balance society in health, literacy, and employment is presumed to build up the self-reliance of our nations in socio-economic parameters in all respects. Education and health programmes will be at the doorstep of the common masses.

With language and other subjects, health and social and environmental science should be given the highest priority during the juvenile period of education, to create a feeling of responsibility for the nation, nature, and the surroundings.

Schooling will be completed with short-term teacher training, midwifery, nursing, sewing, and different compulsory technological career-building training courses for boys and girls as part of school-level education. At the end, the school education certificate, training certificate, and an appointment letter should be presented to everyone on an optional basis to join with the national service group in or around the student's locality, to fulfil national demand. Post-school, tertiary career-building education should be encouraged and should be monitored digitally through the national citizen card.

There should be a national workers' board. All daily and floating workers of the state, irrespective of nation, should be recorded in a regionally based centralised digitalised system, which should control and monitor their daily service and remuneration. Workers, including migrant workers, are the best resource for economic growth and production discipline. Their health and security should be facilitated. There should be national workers' rest houses near the industrial areas, and others to offer them shelter at a low price on a daily basis.

For the resurrection of nations from their disrupted conditions, they need to be reconditioned by increasing utility and demand and by promoting and boosting production and provision. No banking service remodelling will give the desired result. The only way out is by creating consumers and increasing utility and demand, which is possible by spreading money to every hand; this is work at every hand.

Let our nations come under an umbrella of peace and friendly relations. Let our nations look at the crying needs of the citizens' well-being. Let us together save the world from pollution and wastage. In turning away from the basic needs of a nation, self-reliance cannot be reached. A hungry soul can only scream for food, but it becomes dumb when it comes to self-reliance.

CHAPTER ONE

ELEMENTARY

A ROAD MAP FOR POST-CORONA ECONOMIC RECONSTRUCTION

In a time of destruction, create something.
Maxine Hong Kingston

POST-CORONA ECONOMY

The ongoing COVID-19 pandemic outburst embarked on its journey all of a sudden from Wuhan, China, in December 2019. As per Worldometer's data on COVID-19 on the morning of 05/01/2021, at 2.10 GMT the coronavirus had already taken the lives of total number of 18,59,839 in the world, with the morbidity cases of total number 8,60,93,830 people, with a total recovery of 6,10,45,584 people. The highest four countries by rank are the USA in first place with total cases of morbidity is 2,13,53,051; total deaths 3,62,123; and total recoveries are 1,27,36,512. India at second place with a total morbidity cases at 1,03,57,569; total death is 1,49,886; and total recoveries are 99,75,340. Brazil at third place with a total case of morbidity is 77,54,560; total deaths 1,96,591; and total recoveries are 6,875,230 and Russia is at fourth place with a total morbidity cases at 32,60,138; total death is at 58,988 and a total recovery of 26,40,038 people.

The total morbidity rate is still increasing by leaps and bounds. Hopefully, the recovery rate at present is still increasing more than the death record. It is not known when the journey of COVID-19 will stop or be countered and overcome by any powerful medicine.

This book is not politically motivated. It is just from the cry of my spirit, with love and affection for my land and countrymen, and every bit of my heart, with feelings of humanity for the human race. Without any trace of political colour, without any political or national business, and without throwing any political stone at others, I have tried my best to focus on the effect of the coronavirus pandemic (known as COVID-19) on the human race.

It has made the world come to a standstill and caused it to struggle to keep life at whatever pace. Now corona is live, but the world economy is in threat and gradually coming down towards destruction.

It is not weapon that can stop COVID; the only weapon is a medicine that can prevent it and kill it, to save the human race.

The world is bewildered by the sudden attack of the coronavirus. In the absence of suitable preventive and healing medications in the world, countries have started to develop a powerful medicine. COVID-19 has proven that a weapon can affect a certain amount of life, but medicine can save lives and unite the human race. It is the only demand of humanity today.

At present, we are helpless. We, the world, are now on the back foot. We have chosen the method of self-defence in place of resistance. Corona has pushed us to hide our faces behind a piece of cloth, a *mask*. Corona, an unseen virus, has hit the world, which is now bound to hide behind the door in shut houses; this is called a *lockdown* and *shutdown*. We are maintaining distance from each other, under the term *social distancing*, in fear of being tainted.

Corona has made us bound to close the doors of all religious buildings and governing bodies, and it has proven that, it is not a temple, or a church, or a mosque, or any religious house where you can pray for your life. It is only a hospital, where you can pray for life. And with the threat on our lives, corona has established that the real gods and goddesses who can save our lives are doctors, nurses, midwives, and other health workers with white aprons, dedicated to preserving the human race.

COVID-19 has already given us a whiff of its destructive character. With the present and past corona pandemic, the world economy and society are at stake. Corona will stop sometime, but it will destroy the world economy. Already, as I am writing, trade, businesses, transportation, schools, colleges, shops, and institutions have been shut down. Millions of people have lost their income and jobs. All types of production have been stopped. The human race in lockdown is completely messed up; we are at our wits' end.

When corona stops its journey or slows down, we may easily observe the feeble frame of the world economic system and see that countries are struggling for survival. The world powers will have to peep at the post-corona scenario to find out our deficiency. We need to have concentration and control over the deficiencies to get healed and repaired and build up a healthy environment.

Without any political aim, keeping aside all personal prejudice and expectations, I am seeking to highlight the way we can attain the success. To find a permanent solution, the state needs to repair the economy after recurring destruction by restructuring national economic structures and revamping it to give it a fresh face. In doing so, we will be able to create a really potent, self-dependent, healthy, happy nation, without any threat on the economy and with a life of coexistence and of peaceful, healthy, happy international relations worldwide.

The entire world at this time is going through the coronavirus invasion. The COVID-19 pandemic is not confined to an individual country. It has already encroached into almost all nations of the globe. The morbidity rate is really high. It has already disrupted the health and economic systems of the affected states. It is beyond prediction when the world countries will be free from the clutches of the devastating virus. But certainly, it will not easily be controlled like all the other diseases already existing in our society, like the flu, cholera, the plague, smallpox, typhoid, etc.

However, a civilised nation can't sit idle with stupidity and observe the destruction of society at the hands of viruses. We hold the sole option to struggle out of the complex situation and overcome the viruses. We need to make wise, positive, determined, progressive, and winning decisions. We have to repair the loss. We must inspire hope and raise the spirits of our citizens. We have to come out from the corona culture, symbolised by masks, quarantine, social distancing, and lockdown. These indicate fear and surrender.

POST-CORONA ECONOMY

COVID-19 has cruelly made us destitute in income, health, economy, relations, livelihood, and even in our normal social lives and emotions, like passion, love, and self-esteem. It has made us numb. We are terrified and have forgotten to shed a tear for our loved ones dying from coronavirus.

A Claim for Renaissance in Health, Education, and National Economy

No, a nation cannot breathe behind a piece of cloth and look at others with suspense, abhorrence, and fear. We cause to wipe out corona, and all such various already exist and have yet to come to us.

Therefore, our aim should be to wink at and neglect all viruses through our advanced planning of the national lifestyle—a lifestyle that will automatically build us up to be physically protected. This includes inborn physical fitness, total cleanliness, and social education with implementation.

a) **Congenital physical fitness:** If a child turns up with total immunisation, then protection that is powerful against any virus will automatically arise and deliver them from the threat of any virus.
b) **Total cleanliness:** If we can grow a zero-tolerance cleanliness which assures over all cleanliness from house to road by implanting a habit of love for nature and natural resources, then indoor and outdoor

pollution and wastage of natural wealth will automatically decrease and stop.

c) **Social teaching and implementation:** Education from childhood should be nature and socio-health-oriented. It should teach a love for nature, gardening, self-hygiene, waste awareness, healthy habits, cleanliness, etc. Practical application should be part of education.

In this manner, we can make up a really very clean, healthy state that will never succumb to the virus's influence. Physical fitness will protect the body from external risks. A fair society will keep pollution-related hazards away from societal life.

Societies and countries need resurrection in the health and medication system, national and social economy, production, and distribution system.

We should have to be geared up with powerful modern weapons, expert and dedicated soldiers, and wide battlefields, to fight eye to eye with all enemies of human society, like pandemics and viruses. These weapons are not meant to kill but to save the lives of our dear ones. We have to spread and expand battlefields, like health centres and hospitals. We have to increase the number of soldiers, like doctors, nurses, midwives, scientists, pathologists, and health workers.

We need to justify the challenge before us in the present scenario. Corona has presented a challenge to the basic foundations of the human spirit and companionship. Those are (1) health, (2) education, (3) food, and (4) economy and income.

1) **Health:** Threatened. The death rally due to COVID-19 is in full swing, despite measures taken in all aspects.
2) **Education system:** Disrupted and stopped, except digital and online education, which benefits a very minimum group of students.
3) **Food:** Almost all types of production closed and barricaded. The supply chain of essential commodities is severely damaged.
4) **Economy and income:**
   a) The national and international economy is in danger.
   b) The economic infrastructure is dismantled.
   c) Shops and establishments, manufacturing plant, and stores are closed. Common daily markets are restricted to the preparation of food grains and common vegetables.
   d) Production is closed and has been stopped. It is now confined to essential daily consumable commodities, like food grains and veggies. Some food products are available to citizens.
   e) All public vehicles, flights, and rails have stopped operating, excluding emergency vehicles and flights.
   f) Income has reached its lowest, which is life-threatening to middle- and lower-income

groups. The unemployment rate has increased manyfold worldwide.

Unemployment

The COVID-19 pandemic has suddenly forced an unexpected and obligatory closure and cessation of work in all types of business establishments, including shops and grocery stores. It has caused a steady rise in unemployment worldwide.

a) Suspension of work in manufacturing houses, shops, various industries, transportation, and civil and construction works has caused millions to go into unemployment.
b) Millions were laid off to manage non-production and the threat of fiscal loss.
c) There are cases of wilful unemployment; the workers leave the organisations at their own risk in fear of failing.
d) Millions of daily and seasonal workers in their home states and migrants to and from other countries have lost jobs. The workers are not interested in going back to their old job, due to feelings of insecurity in life.

Unemployment is growing in new generation in natural way on regular basis. Thus, the overall cumulative figure for unemployment throughout the globe is very alarming.

To get away from the trauma of corona's destruction of normal life and the national economy, a multifaced economic explosion is inevitable. Society, as well as the world economy, is now waiting for resurrection and a renaissance. It is a renaissance in education, a renaissance in health and medication, and also a renaissance in work and production—an all-out growth in the economic organisation of the rural area and lifestyle.

Yes, it is technically possible. It is possible only by increasing production and the consumers. Printing new notes is not a solution. Donations, help, relief, or assistance in kind or money can never be a solution. A country can't run or survive on unproductive assistance. It never boosts an economy; rather, it invites disgrace, and ultimately, the nation is prefixed by the term *poor*. National and international organisations can help, donate to, or assist a country, but that will never give self-dependence. It will grow insecurity in society. It will ultimately cause human beings to be inactive, and it may admit dependence. It may also raise a 'behavioural pollution' that will smear the entire society.

Only self-reliance, in the way of very substantial, honest, and powerful economic progress and development, utilising dedicated, prepared, and healthy national manpower and resources, can build up a satisfying, powerful, and smart economy and country.

To revive the distressed economy, nations need a speedy recovery in the production site. We have to go ahead with three major processes to fight against the downfall of the national economy.

1) Foremost, we have to bring out fear from the minds of citizens by bringing health and medical benefits to their doorsteps.
2) The economy of a country depends and moves on growth in production. Thus, the administration should emphasise the growth and spread production.
3) The country needs to increase national production and the consumers—in other words, the buyers—to strengthen the economic condition of the country. That will increase and hold the balance of utility, demand, production, and use of goods and services.

The present economic system needs to regenerate and restructure production systematically and positively, keeping in mind that health, education, and work are the rights of all. These are all the prime needs for life to be achieved at all. They have to be spread amongst all citizens of the state. Increasing salaries is not the solution or positive idea to bring change in national output growth. Only spreading of salaries amongst citizens is the concrete, logical, and positive solution. It is the sole path to creating more and more consumers, and the primary way of increasing yield. It will bring a growth in utility and demand that will ultimately push up consumption and production. A completely neck-and-neck balanced economy in the long run is deserved or is expected. In this direction, the national economy will move towards positive and zero-balance growth.

As much as we can grow consumers, in return we may get growth in production. Increasing the consumers depends on passing around money in the hands of the consumers. Spreading of money amongst hands means an increase of workers, which is, in the basic sense, an increase of employment. To make a strong economy, we thus need to give jobs to every workable hand.

Corona has not killed human beings alone; it has severely twisted nations' economic structures and pointed out the oddities and evils in our cultural and behavioural attitudes and attacked our social atmosphere. It has given us a lesson to purify our nature and atmosphere. We have reached the extreme point of our stupidity. We need a dedicated national force to rebuild a pollution-free, clean-air society. Let the younger generation work and earn after completing the schooling period and serve the country for a certain period, until they are suitably placed in a job. Let the new generation hold the flag of cleanliness and purification of nature and atmosphere by active participation, for the success of the Save Nature, Save the World programme, and boost feelings of nationality in being a member of a national service group.

CHAPTER TWO

COVID-19 PRE-, PRESENT, POST- (PPP)

ECONOMIC REVIEW AND RESURRECTION

The human body has been designed to resist an infinite number of changes and attacks brought about by its environment. The secret of good health lies in successful adjustment to changing stresses on the body.
Harry J. Johnson

POST-CORONA ECONOMY

We today need to have a look at the past, present, and future scenarios of the national and international economy, i.e. world economy, in respect of the COVID-19 outbreak and its impact on human civilisation.

Most of the countries in the world have come into existence through a great deal of struggle and bloodshed, and have also fought through several social and political crises; ultimately, they have proven their existence in world politics and the world economic system.

There is a history of civil wars, natural disasters, floods, droughts, epidemics, pandemics, quakes, etc. that have claimed lives in countries worldwide. A list of the death toll from epidemics and pandemics is given below.

Table No. 1

Sl.No.	PERIOD	NAME/DISEASE	PLACE/ORIGIN & Migrated to.	DEATH TOLL
1	3000 BC	HAMIN MANGHA/ Epedemic	China village	Un known
2	430 bc	Plegue of Athens		100000
3	165-180 AD	Antonine Plegue		5 million
4	250-271 AD	Plegue of Cyprian		1 million
5	541-542 AD	Plegue of Justirian		30-50 million
6	735-737 AD	Japanese smallpox		1 million
7	1315-17 AD	BLACK DEATH/ Influenja	China,England & Wales	15 % OF population
8	1346-53 AD		Southern England, Northerb Britain & Scandanevia	75-200 million/ 10-60% of population
9	1629-1631		Northern Italy	280000
10	1656 1657		Rome, southern italy	150000

		DEATH TOLL FROM NATURAL EPIDEMICS & PANDEMICS IN WORLD		
11	1817-1824	1 st Cholera outbreak	Jessore, India, Sri Lanka, indonesia, Thyland (Java) etc	100000
12	1829-1837	2 nd Cholora outbreak	US & Canada	17000+
13	1831		Hangary	100000
14			Egypt	130000
15	1832		UK	55000
16			London	6536
17	1833		Paris	20000
18			France	100000
19	1846	3 rd Cholora outbreak	Russia	1 million
20			Mecca	15000
21	1848		England and Wells	52000
22	1849		London	14137
23	1852-1860		Asia, Europe N. Africa, America, Grate Britain	23000
24	1863-1875	Cholera 4th	Bengal, Hungary	190000
25	1881-1896	Cholera 5th	Hamburg	1.5% of population
26	1889-1890	Asian flu		1million
27	may 1889	Russian flu		30000
28	1899-1923	Cholera 6th	India	.5 Million
29	1991		Paru	3000
30	1910-1911	6th Cholera epedimic		800000
31	1918	Influenza /Pandemic	World countries	20-50 million
32	1991	7th Cholera	Peru	3000
33	2008-2009	Cholera	Zimbabuea	4200
34	2017	Cholera	Somalia & Yemen	2000
35	2019 -2020	COVID-19-Corona Pendemic	Wuhan/ China World countries	As on sate-

Listed in this chart are natural disasters that caused many deaths, with causes and locations mentioned where available, from 3000 BC to today. It is found that from the ancient period, viral epidemics and pandemics have taken lives and destroyed civilisations. Historians and travellers then could not set and did not clearly cite the causes of the deaths. Nevertheless, the symptoms they wrote in their records and writings make it clear that the viral attacks, followed by natural disasters, were the grounds of destruction.

The same things still break out in different countries, in new formations and with new symptoms. Cholera, influenza, the plague, poxes, etc. are still active. The only difference is in the health scheme. Some pandemics have stopped, and we can't say when those will once again erupt like volcanoes over society. COVID-19, the ongoing pandemic, will also be terminated. Humans will become immunised to challenge the virus. But like with past pandemics, new viruses will come. All these things are uncertain and painful, but it is part of the reality of life.

Corona

Pre-, Present, Post- (PPP) Scenarios

Today we will go over the scenario of our static countries with stable and strong economies around the globe. COVID-19, a horrifying, strange pandemic, with its complete invasive nature, suddenly fell on the human race and wrecked the social and economic structures of nations throughout the world.

Pre-COVID-19

All the little and large countries around the world were going about their peaceful days with common political, economic, and social agendas. As per usual, some difference of opinion on various issues was going on and just about topics that were going to be resolved peacefully. I don't wish to bring up political subjects here, because world history says these are unavoidable. That signified that the world was at a normal stage. We were in a passive and positive mood.

COVID-19 at Present

The present COVID-19 scenario is alarming. We can't imagine, what we have to experience in long run, because a small invisible virus has destroyed our social structure. It has ravaged the all-powerful economy of the world and disrupted the social and physical health of nations. We have no powerful weapon with which to obliterate a small invisible virus. We have no powerful weapon with which to deliver the human race, called medicine. Thus, we have been ruined by the threat of a small strange virus.

Arms and ammunition can be utilised to preserve our sovereignty. It may save us from the threat of atomic weapons and other fatal weapons. However, we have yet to find a weapon that will save the human race from fatal diseases and viruses, though from the inception of human society in ancient days, humans have also faced unseen killers in the form of epidemics and pandemics that destroyed and ruined society.

POST-CORONA ECONOMY

We are just playing hide-and-seek with COVID-19. It is because we have no powerful medicine ready to challenge corona. Thus, we have hidden behind shut curtains and let corona travel freely until it dies on its own. We have placed it under the well-dressed terms *lockdown* and *social distancing*.

When nations were behind closed doors, our great, dedicated doctors boldly faced the corona threat, sacrificing their every moment to cure the human race in spite of having very minimum lifesaving kits for their own safety. It is not just us, the Indians; the entire world will never forget their sacrifice and service to the nations. We must try to understand our helplessness and our priority at the initial stage.

COVID-19 has compelled us to face how all the lifelines of powerful nations collapsed within a couple of days. National and international social structures were brought down and broken up. Our life is now at stake with the outbreak of devastating Corona virus.

All schools, colleges, and social, cultural, and religious institutes and their activities have been closed down. National and multinational establishments have suspended their normal daily activities and have shortened their operating hours and have started running their work from home.

Trade and business activities, common markets, and shops for daily consumables are closed all over different countries. Workshops and factories are closed, and productions stopped.

Millions of employees worldwide have lost their jobs. Related to the closure of workshops and factories and due to the cessation of work in the civil and infrastructural sectors, millions of daily and contractual workers worldwide have lost businesses, food, funds, and shelter.

Flights, railways, and private and public transport have been suspended in fear of the spread of the pandemic. Fear of dying, loss of work, rise in unemployment, and the stop of human mobility have destroyed social structures and the culture of human order. National and international economic structures have taken on an alarming new shape.

Notwithstanding, we Indians and other countrymen are likely to outlast the grip of the corona pandemic, despite our weak medical facilities. We are blessed, because we hold in our society thousands of alive 'ladies with the lamps', great mothers and sisters like Florence Nightingale, and great, dedicated doctors, fighting eye to eye against the coronavirus. We will never forget the excellent service of the doctors and the nurses in the hospitals, the 'temples of life'.

The poor condition of our national and international health programme is coming in front of us. COVID-19 has stopped the entire human civilisation. But we can't be defeated by the virus. We have to endure; we have to conquer it. We need to keep hold of our hope, to wipe away the evil power, and to wisely and steadily overcome the PANIC—i.e., pathos, anxiety, negativity, instinct, and challenge.

Post-COVID-19

Corona has disrupted the entire human civilisation. Lockdowns, shutdowns, quarantine, social distancing, wearing masks, staying home, sanitising hands regularly, sanitising virus-affected areas, etc.—several types of measures have been taken to save countrymen from the intense force of the corona pandemic. Physicians and nurses, along with health assistance staff, are dedicatedly fighting to heal patients. Corona pandemic is spreading drastically in human localities. Scientists are engaged in inventing a medicine to heal patients and in discovering a preventive to protect the common people from the pandemic and contamination.

We know that scientists somewhere in the world will discover the cure. Corona will be defeated. But when? The death toll is increasing rapidly throughout the world.

But we shall overcome.

Yes, we shall overcome someday. But how long do we wait for this? When will we take a deep breath of relaxation? Even I cannot say, if I am fortunate enough to escape the clutches of corona virus, and survive. No, it is not me; it is the thought of millions and millions of people in the world.

The world countries are desperately searching for a medicine to kill the virus and its effects. Doctors, scientists, and chemists around the globe are engaged to invent medicines to kill corona immediately. We can, and it will be in our hands very shortly. But we will not get back the loved ones we have lost.

Now in the days post-COVID-19, we need to find ways to protect our country, to eliminate the causes of our failure, and to rectify, improve, and strengthen them.

We all have to survive. We must recover the health of the country in all fields of life and whatever corona has toppled and destroyed.

We have to restore economic health. We have to restructure our health planning and programmes. We have to reinstate our mobility, business, and trade. We have to get our schools, colleges, and all educational establishments into full swing. We can't stop until or unless we once again see our innocent kids cavorting in the green surface of nature outside our homes.

Thus, the post-corona health revival package should be permanent, positive, and systematic, so that we can overcome such troubles easily.

Health Is Wealth

First and foremost, we must restructure our family wellness programme and make a very powerfully equipped medical and health service system all over the country that will ensure a complete wellness package for countrymen, from childhood to old age and even to death.

POST-CORONA ECONOMY

Corona is not the last enemy for us. We know we have to wait for a more powerful 'death sentence' in this world again and again, with a new figure, a new colour, a new dress, and a raw form. Whether we admit it or not, we should accept that. We modern human beings are knowingly or unknowingly creating the viruses with our living habits.

Furthermore, corona will not go away entirely, because a virus never dies. Any virus, either powerful or weak, can find safe shelter within a human torso in latent condition and burst out from time to time. It's all natural. Thus, we could not completely stop smallpox, typhoid, cholera, the plague, the flu, etc. Those once destroyed many civilisations and claimed millions of lives, in India and world countries. Corona will also remain dormant within us and may erupt like a volcano at any time.

To save the entire human civilisation from such epidemics and pandemics, existing or new, I believe from the core of my heart that the best way of treating it is to *care for and treat the patient, not the disease.* If we can make our people healthy persons, human society will be healthy, and no disease will conquer a healthy human force. It should be started from childhood.

Now we have to be ready in advance with internal and external ways to fight against viruses and all such diseases. The viruses infect comparatively low-immunity and weak human bodies. So our motto and target should be strengthening the immunity and physical fitness of all.

If we become successful in belling the cat, we will require minimum medical support throughout life, which implies it will be a comparatively lesser medical expenditure burden on the state. We need to adopt a full-scale health system for the new born babies and all.

To extend to everyone in every distant corner of the rural areas, we will have to strengthen and distribute the medical scheme. We need to make space for all types of medications and medical theories still alive. We have to encourage and patronise the all-natural and chemical medication processes and theories by application and research to treat everybody.

As much as we will depend on a limited system for treatment, it will become costlier to low- and middle-income groups. We have to reach and spread all medicinal systems to provide health service to all at a low price. The medicines, either allopathy, homoeopathy, Ayurveda, or different natural therapies, such as acupuncture, acupressure, etc.—all theories were generated after research by the inventors, and the basic components of the medicine are naturally only applied in a different form and way.

Education

We have to restructure our education system also to boost our national strength.

POST-CORONA ECONOMY

COVID-19 has already compelled our children to remain within the home. As per World Health Organization (WHO), children up to ten years of age are highly vulnerable targets of contamination of the dreadful virus. The stay-home theory has been applied to children, and all other junior and senior students, irrespective of class and age, are confined within four walls. Only a very minimal number of schools and colleges have started online and digital education on an experimental basis. Practically every country does not have enough capability to maintain such arrangements and experiences.

We therefore require a new national education system to spread education at the root level from childhood, and we have to wipe out the habit of leaving and dropping school, which is a common occurrence in primary and junior school levels. Leaving school happen due to poverty and social components. We have to wind out the barriers wisely so that the family as a whole feels the importance of training to survive in life, for progress socially and financially.

It is not God in any form in the nations that can set up and preserve the human race. God is unitary of our mental spirit and ability. With my belief in God and goddesses, I want to say, our worship and our offerings to our God and goddesses should be through EEE—i.e., our utmost enthusiasm, education, and endeavours. It will give us the boon of an educated, smart society.

To make a smart human society, we have to spread education at the grassroots level. When a pupil does not reach towards education, education should reach towards the pupil. When a student does not reach towards school, the school should reach towards the student. We have to spread education, like health, to the remote villages and rural countries in an advanced new form. Where parents cannot send their child to school, due to occupation in the cultivation of land or in the workshop, the school will move close to the land or workshop so that the working parents can ensure their child is safe and learning lessons in front of them. The farmer or the worker will gain energy in their work. It presents a country with many benefits, like (a) a happy and healthy society, (b) better cultivation, (c) high production, (d) growth in national economy, (e) a smart society, and (f) a chance to more easily reach a zero-illiteracy society.

Employment

Our next challenge is employment. COVID-19's worst attack is on the nations' fundamental economic structure. That consists of trade and business. If we closely observe, we may consider a very pitiful scenario. In economic terms, the people in the production phase are known as (a) entrepreneurs, (b) businessmen, (c) management, (d) traders, and (e) workers. The same people in the consumption phase are called (a) owners and stockists, (b) sellers, (c) consumers, and (d) buyers.

The production phase and consumption cum utility phase would maintain very safe and cordial relations to produce better products and higher gross revenue. No doubt, we all are human beings, and unquestionably, there are also different opinions on salaries, wages, etc. in the production part and on the prices, quality, and weight of consumable goods in the consumption part. But even so, there was a really good understanding amongst all.

The coronavirus disrupted all relations and understanding within a few days. Every bit of an infected body collapse, from top to toe, and COVID-19 has likewise infected the entire human society and harshly rolled its bulldozer over the world economy.

The production division was bound to stop production, and the obvious solution was to close the doors of production houses and shops. The obvious answer was the suspension of work; the result of it was the end of the careers of men and women of different views and staff grades worldwide. At the same time, millions of salaried workers and daily workers cum labourers in every business sector in different countries have suddenly been marked as unemployed. Even native workers who depend on wages earned by contract, daily wages, or wages earned on a temporary contract basis are now in a critical situation. They have lost their daily essentials of livelihood, like income, shelter, and food. Migrant workers are therefore now a larger menace to the national economy.

The threat of death from corona has locked and closed production houses; production houses have ceased production. Non-production has stopped income and business. The decision to stop business has trended and stopped the jobs of workers and labourers. So, the ultimate result is the excessive rise in unemployment—in clear words, stop of *income*. At the same time, due to the closure of all business establishments, markets, and workshops, the sales of commodities are held back. The earnings and wages of the workers are a percentage of the net income of the clientele. If the business can't generate earnings, how will it pay the salaries and wages of the workers and labourers?

Thus, income of producer, workers of all level are stopped or reduced due to the corona disaster. With the worker being a constituent of a family, family income is brought down or discontinued. Thus, the total living standard with the economic structure of the country, as well as of society, is disrupted. I elaborately discussed this to bring up some essential details to look at.

Who is responsible for the increase of millions and millions of people in unemployment all of a sudden? It is not the producer or the entrepreneur. It is COVID-19.

From a kid to an old person, each and every person plays a direct and indirect role in the development of production and the economic system. Even the status, sex, age, and preference and taste of the inhabitants of a region influence the regional business environment. Utility and demand also influence the types of production. For instance, where there is no electricity, the inhabitants will search for kerosene lamps or candles, not a bulb or refrigerator or other electrical appliances. Every product has its users and consumers; thus, the consumables are influenced by the types of users of the region.

Total economic growth depends on utility, demand, and consumption. So, to revive our national economic health, we have to reinstate the lost working environment. Even in a fairer way we have to regain economic health of the country. We must have to boost total consumption by increasing utility, demand, consumption, and expenditure (UDCE), i.e., buying power. That will, in turn, force the increase of the chain of production, appointment, utility, demand, consumption, and expenditure (PAUDEC).

The Production Chain

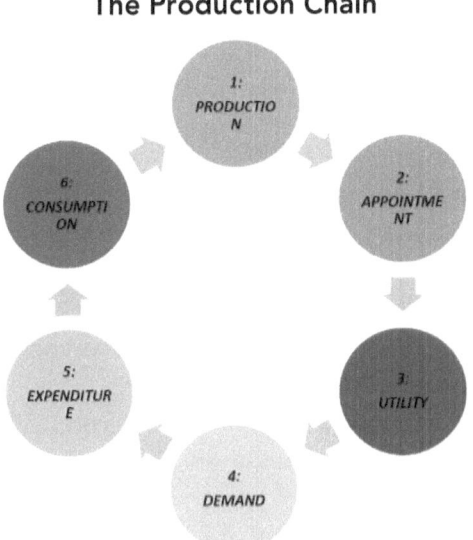

The economic growth is completely dependent on production and consumption. Consumption depends on income. The spending power of people has suddenly dropped. We have to overcome the situation. In turn, to increase economic power, we have to generate or confirm income growth.

The Economic Power Growth Cycle

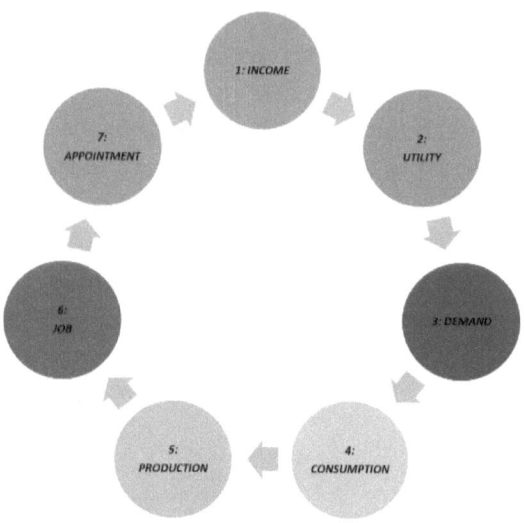

To strengthen national economic growth, nations have to spread IUDCPJA. The cycle will start with income. Income will generate utility of a product, and the utility will create demand. Demand will influence more consumption, consumption will boost production, and production will initiate a demand for more work or jobs. The jobs will compel an increase in manpower and appointments. The cycle of IUDCPJA will automatically influence to strengthen the economy of a country.

Please note that I have used the term *spread* in place of *increase*. Yes, my view may create great discomfort and disapproval in a group of existing employees. But this approach is not to remove or lock the salaries of the employees anyway. Only my proposal will increase the income of a household.

We have to deeply observe and realise the factor.

The growth in the number of employees may increase the number of income heads, and more income heads will create more consumers. They will, in turn, come to the IUDCPJA circle to keep the balance of the common theory of demand and supply. That is a step to building up a stable and strong economy.

Whether we accept it or not, the low- to medium-income groups maintain the development of the national economy by spending. These groups of workers spend the majority of their income, and this is the primary cash flow of the common daily market. These groups mainly create a negative income that influences the bank directly but easily. These low- to medium-income groups of workers help to generate the bank's fund source through various bank loans. This is one component of the source of a bank's profit.

Each of these groups is a direct creator of consumption. So increase in this group is increase in consumption units, and that contributes to the production unit of consumables.

The high-income group also consumes the same products, leaving a major portion of their earning for savings, which indirectly stops money flow in the market.

We have to consider that the consumer needs and habits of humanity are very common to the rich and poor. The principal things we require in life are the same. It only differs in quality and brand. We cannot consume more than we need; we can only eat costlier items and use costlier commodities. A low- or middle-income man can buy rice at a low price from the market, for more or less thirty-five rupees per kilogram, whereas a high-income man will purchase high-priced rice for like fifty-six to sixty rupees per kilogram, or more. In the same way, high-income people will purchase branded apparel, branded food, etc., whilst others will purchase from the standard marketplace. This difference in spending habits creates a very small percentage of higher living costs for the higher-income group.

This high-income group spends their money on costly household gadgets, like a branded AC, fridge, or washing machine; on eats; and on ornaments. Yet they save a greater percentage of their income in other ways, like by purchasing bonds, making fixed deposits, etc. Meanwhile, the low- and middle-income groups mostly struggle to keep family expenditure under control and solve their problems in the way of bank loans. This produces negative income. They can hardly save money. It would be better to say that they save disguised financial burdens. Because, the person fights to save a minimum percentage of income in account, on the other hand, he receives a loan balance with a fixed interest that is payable monthly.

What is the social and economic effect of the income of both groups?

The low- to middle-income groups create maximum positive consumption. Their expenditure keeps the common marketplace alive. They are the largest source of monetary resources for marketing and generating liquid cash flow. They never create idle money. The low- and middle-income groups, being the greatest in quantity of any country, consume the majority of consumable goods. They are the controllers of GNP and GDP.

As per the economic theory of demand and supply, when demand pushes supply, it will push production, and yield will push for the addition of labour for output. This will push employment. This employment will again create a new circle.

High-income groups of employees being proportionately very small in a country, they occupy a comparatively little space in direct resourcing the cash flow to the common market. Though they are bigger source of funding for the Bank.

They are the primary buyers of interest-based paper money, like fixed deposits, term deposits, shares, etc. And as per the banking system, a certain percent of money collected from the investors is further used to make money. This accumulated money is endowed by the bank to businessmen for businesses and production homes. In the long run, this strengthens the national and international economic system.

Both possess a substantial influence on the internal economic system. The low- to middle-income group has maximum direct influence and impact in reducing the unemployment rate of a nation by way of making many production possibilities in the marketplace. On the other hand, the higher-income group creates a set of idle, low-productivity stagnant funds that can't roll in the market daily like liquid money. The higher-income group spends a lot of finances to buy gold and amber decorations, luxuries, and fashion products that deliver a comparatively lesser impact and influence in building a nation, as well as a national economic system.

Hence, to develop a country, we need to create an economic system where we may boldly *spread* salary rather than *increase* it. There is perhaps no negative possibility in the economic development of a rural area, as well as the world. It simply must have very positive and a good impact on society.

A) There is a good share of unemployed young people throughout the land. When employment increases, it will benefit all families who are waiting for a job for their family members. This will benefit the families financially, mentally, and socially, and help them become a happy family, free from stress and poverty.

B) Unemployment is now a curse on our society. COVID-19 has drastically run its bulldozer over the world economy and has suddenly increased the millions and millions of unemployment cases in the countries along with the previous existing unemployment burden. To overcome this trial, we have to move forward with the intention to rebuild our nation with work, employment, and training. This will be a more progressive way to counter this crisis.

C) Whatever the education standards, all boys and girls need some financial support to maintain their basic daily needs. When it is not at hand, in an effort to come up with money, they will desperately attempt to obtain it in whatever way. This desperate mentality in people, especially on young generation ultimately vitiate the morality and atmosphere of the society, as well as spoil the social structure. The rise in employment will bring down the uncertainty and help create a moral, smart ideal nation.

D) Every new opportunity for employment has some social impact on human life. Money power helps increase change in the literacy, health and cultural progress. This ultimately builds an ideal social atmosphere as a whole.

E) A happy society is the strength of a country. The younger generation makes up the greatest percentage and is the strength of a nation. They are the devoted soldiers of a nation because of social and national security. But a demoralised, broken-hearted young group can ruin a nation more quickly than any weapon. Thus, to rebuilt our nation, ideal in all respect, employment for all must be carried out. It is a means of survival for the human race.

F) There was a time when the uptake of products, i.e., spending money for goods, was considered the best method to establish a strong economy whilst savings were a shameful thing. But day by day and step by step, modern life has changed and polished all theories and conceptions into a new shape.

Thus, the savings is now an integral part of fiscal health of an employee's family life. The concept of savings with a target of family safety in future has made employees interested. The financial establishments, business organisations like bank, Insurance agencies, etc. has come out with various attractive savings options to cater the earning people.

G) Savings are now the strength of a nation and are likewise a large weapon to strengthen the economic and social structure of a nation. The emphasis on employment to build up safe and wide consumers' strength in the market will by no means disturb the savings accumulation; instead, it may boost the savings. The more we spread our income head in our country the more we increase our consumption of merchandise and the more we spread our savings head. It will automatically increase the national GDP rate and strengthen the internal economic system.

Is it possible to give employment to a whole country? Yes, it is. It is within our existing capacity and economy by a judicious application of state-building policy, with honourable, active, and sincere effort through a smooth financial restructure and reconstruction. The great potential of the country is manpower. When the total manpower will work together, a growth in production and income will generate an explosion in the GDP and GNP of the country.

CHAPTER THREE

LET ME LIVE

TOWARDS A POLLUTION-FREE SOCIETY

Happiness is not in the mere possession of money; it lies in the joy of achievement, in the thrill of creative effort.

Franklin D. Roosevelt

Pollution is a silent killer of the human race and nature. It has the overwhelming power to spread diseases and kill humans of all ages. It can destroy society, directly and indirectly. Air pollution directly affects the environment and spreads chronic diseases. It is not only an enemy of the human race; it is unsparing. It can destroy society, the environment, culture, and also sculptures. We have already seen the destruction of many ancient archaeological sculptures and buildings around the world. From the old days, we have been facing a great problem with pollution. We have lost beauty of our nature; we have lost thousands of birds, beasts, trees, and blossoms, and we are continuing to lose the beauty of nature. To preserve our earth and restore ecological balance, fighting against pollution is a must.

The following table has a few mortality records of pollution-related diseases in the world and the total number of patients suffering from these diseases, living with personalised medicine and medical support, and living a very restricted life, with the threat of death.

Table No. 2

Mortality and live patient rate of pollution-related diseases. (In Million)			
Mortality rate				Live
Diseases Name & Year	2000	2010	2017	2017
High blood pressure	7.93	9.08	10.44	217.96
Smoking	6.35	6.57	7.1	182.48
Air pollution Total	4.71	4.76	4.9	147.42
High Blood sugar	4.32	5.48	6.53	170.57
Child wasting	2.53	1.59	1.08	90.99
Outdoor Air Pollution	2.55	3.04	3.41	83.05
Indoor Air Pollution	2.31	1.87	1.64	59.47
Alcohol	2.35	2.68	2.84	NA
Unsafe water source	1.73	1.48	1.23	63.89
Low Birthweight	1.71	1.38	1.1	NA
Cardiovascular disease	13.7	15.62	12.79	36587
Neonatal disorder	2.66	2.21	1.78	18578
Leaver Disease	1.05	1.19	1.32	41.4
Digestive Disorder	1.92	2.14	2.38	85.29
Diarrhea	2.13	1.86	1.57	NA
Malnutrition	8.84	4.59	3.32	NA
Cancer	6.91	813	9.56	233.51
Respiratory Disease	3.59	3.52	3.91	112.32
Tuberculosis	1.62	1.32	1.18	NA

Classification of pollution is not important; we need to stop pollution, with the priority of giving a healthy life to our society. It is extremely important, because pollution is everywhere around us, affecting nature day by day and destroying the ecological equilibrium of the world. This crime against the world's beauty and purity is being caused by the human race.

POST-CORONA ECONOMY

Our abuse of it and attitude in consuming it now has us threatened by the scarcity of natural resources. The earth has gifted us with a colourful life. In return, we humans have presented it with pollution, poison, and destruction. Ascribable to our recklessness and absence of foresight, we are breaking down our sustainable energies, for which our successors must have to stand. They might have to face life risks soon—and severely.

Pollution is now a great silent killer of the human race. In the year 2019, as per the IQAir World Air Quality Report 2019, Bangladesh, with a total population of 166,368,149, was the most air-polluted country, with an average air pollution level of 97.1 in 2018 and 83.3 in 2019.

Table No. 3

WORLD'S MOST POLLUTED COUNTRIES & AVARAGE POLLUTION RATE			
COUNTRY	POPULATION	2018	2019
BANGLADESH	166368149	97.1	83.3
PAKISTAN	200813818	74.27	65.8
MONGOLIA	3121772	58.5	62
AFGHANISTAN	36373176	61.8	58.8
INDIA	1354051854	72.54	58.1
INDONESIA	266794980	42.01	51.7
BAHRAIN	1566993	59.8	46.8
NEPAL	29624035	54.15	44.5

Table No. 4

WORLD'S MOST AIR POLLUTED CITIES AND AVERAGE POLLUTION RATE: UNIT- µg/m3					HIGHEST POLLUTION	
CITIES	COUNTRY	2017	2018	2019	POLLUTION	TIME
GHAZIABAD	INDIA	144.6	135.2	110.2	235.9	December
HORTON	CHINA	116.0	116.0	110.1	189.1	March
GUJRANWALA	PAKISTAN	NA	106.3	106.3	220.4	January
FAISALABAD	PAKISTAN	NA	130.4	104.6	226.2	December
DELHI	INDIA	108.2	98.6	113.5	200.7	November

Pakistan, with a total population of 200,813,818, was second, with an average air pollution rate of 74.27 in 2018 and 65.81 in 2019. Then after Mongolia and Afghanistan, India, my country, was the fifth in highest air pollution, with an average pollution level of 72.54 in 2018 and 58.1 in 2019.

It is worth noting that amongst the five most air-polluted cities in the world, Ghaziabad, a city of India, ranked first, with the highest pollution rate at 235.9 in December and 144.6 on average in 2017 and 110.2 in 2019. Delhi ranked fifth, with an average of 108.2 in 2017 and 98.6 in 2019, with the highest record of 200.7 in November. A total of two cities in India were in the top five, and a total of twenty-six cities were in the fifty most air-polluted cities in the world. Fourteen states in China and six states in Pakistan were also in the fifty most polluted states. Hotan of China was the second most air-polluted city, with an average pollution rate of 110.1 and the highest at 189.1 in March.

The second most polluted country was Pakistan, with an average pollution of 74.27 in 2018 and 65.81 in 2019. Gujranwala and Faisalabad were the third and fourth most polluted cities, with average pollution rates of 105.3 and 104.6 in 2019 and the highest levels of pollution at 220.4 in January and 226.2 in December.

The earth has gifted us with natural resources to live on. But we human beings, in return, gifted the earth with pollution through our reckless and arbitrary habits.

If we think that natural resources are available in abundance on earth and under the ground, then we are dwelling in a fool's paradise.

Human society has to understand that nature has not yielded all to consume alone. Even nature has not given mankind immortality. Nature has gifted all its riches to share amongst all mankind, so it has given us a short lifespan to share the space with the next generation. We should be prudent. We need to control our consuming behaviour towards natural resources.

The coronavirus has also taught us that pollution is more grievous than a virus. It is a bitter truth that COVID-19 has given new life to the world. We can immediately see the white and clear sky with the bright, shining sun and the beautiful moon with her smiling expression.

We have seen tortoises on lonesome seashores and crocodiles on paths. Wild animals, like tigers and lions, have been moving out of the forest. Peacocks, deer, and various animals have come out of their shelters in the wild and have been meeting under the clear sky. That proves that nature is today taking happy pollution-free breaths. All the polluted cities in India and around the world that were facing disastrous levels of air pollution are now under control. Corona has taught us that if we can refrain from the unnecessary use of natural resources, we can create a healthy and pollution-free environment. It will not require millions of funds to get rid of pollution. We only need a fundless endeavour and awareness to not utilise much of the natural resources, like oils, gases, etc.

We have to consume sustainable energies and natural resources wisely and carefully, to sustain the ecological balance. COVID-19 has punished us for our recklessness, but the bitter truth is that it has also gifted us with comparatively better, pollution-free nature; clean water in the ocean; and a dust-free, clean sky and ever-present sunshine over the earth, with overall clean, healthy air.

As per specialists, corona at present is in its adolescent phase and is spreading its weblike trap everywhere, like a spider, and we don't know when it will stop its journey.

Even so, we can merely hope for what we want. With the cost of Covid-19 massacre, we have been granted a substantial pollution-free world. We ask to respect it and to maintain it, and at the same time, we need to restore the health of our economic and social structure, with a clean and better shape, to defeat all the risks we are yet to face. We may try our best to be equipped with possible weapons, like (1) a well-balanced production and food distribution scheme (in short, food for all); (2) a zero-balance health, immunisation, and medication system (in short, health for all); (3) a well-structured complete education system (in short, education for all); and (4) a well-controlled population, friendlier and healthier national work culture, and a work distribution system for all (in short, employment for all).

Will human beings be controlled by pollution, or will human beings take control over pollution? It's a billion-dollar question for the civilised human world. Pollution is the greatest threat to life in the human universe, and human beings are solely responsible for creating it. Nature has its recycling process and did not create pollution. We civilised human beings are creating pollution through our careless use of natural gifts. Therefore, the banishment of pollution is the duty of the human race.

If we closely observe, we may find that nature, in the natural process, consumes its waste and gives birth of new trees, such as when the leaves of trees fall. Trees fall, and they crash down on to the earth. By a natural process with the influence of rain and wind the leaves and woods, etc. becomes decomposed. It generates its food, called natural manures, to grow more and more. It creates oxygen and carbon dioxide, as per its need. The fruits drop down to the earth and spread seeds, and in some cases, pollen is transported by insects or the wind to make more. Unfortunately, we human beings, through abuse and misuses, have been polluting our environment and atmosphere.

Human civilisation is under the threat of hundreds of human-influenced viruses. To escape the death trap, human society needs to keep nature and biodiversity alive and pollution-free. Humankind must discover the ecological balance by maintaining our natural resources—land, forests, agriculture, minerals, and the animal kingdom (including insects and birds and all living creatures), along with water, air, etc. Nature demands remedial as well as positive attention to maintain the ecological balance. Nature expects our attention, justice, and forethought so it can continue to provide our life support.

Essential ecological balance and biodiversity can be maintained through our deliberate scientific and logical utilisation of abundant natural resources.

The total population's needs are being ministered to by the natural resources available to us. The total area of our world is 510,072 million square kilometres, out of which a total 148,940 million square kilometres are islands and a total 361,132 million square kilometres is water. The world's population is mostly dependent on the total land area.

In this world, only 29% is land area, and 71% is water. Out of the 29% land area, 71% (104 million square kilometres) is usable for human beings. Of that, 19% (28 million square kilometres) is barren land, and 10% (19 million square kilometres) is comprised of glaciers. Out of the remaining 71% of habitable land, 50% (51 million square kilometres) is agricultural land, 37% (39 million square kilometres) is dense forest area, 11% (12 million square kilometres) is shrub area, and 1% (1.5 million square kilometres) is covered in freshwater ponds, lakes, and rivers. The balance of 1% (1.5 million square kilometres) is urban and building area. Out of the total agricultural land of 51 million square kilometres, 77% (40 million square kilometres) is being used for poultry, meat, and dairy purposes. The remaining 23% (11 million square kilometres) is used for crop cultivation.

Out of the 71% (326 million cubic metres) of water area, 97% (320 million cubic metres) is saltwater. It is comprised of oceans. The balance of only 3% (6 million cubic metres) of water area is freshwater. Out of this 3%, 2.5% is unobtainable. These areas are under glaciers, polar ice caps, and the soil. Hence, that only leaves 0.5% of clean water for all world citizens. It is estimated that only approximately 8.4 million litres of water are available for each person on earth.

The quantity of natural resources is decreasing due to our reckless use of them. Moreover, agricultural land is diminishing day by day, due to soil erosion and degradation by natural processes, like rising tides, storms, etc.; man-made erosion caused by deforestation; encroachment of land for industrialisation; and poisoning of agricultural land from draining industrial wastes and chemicals. Food security is falling to an alarming level because of such land degradation. Agricultural land should be wisely managed. Pollution should be stopped. The earth should be revived, with fresh pollution-free air, water, and nature.

To be up to the goal of a pollution-free, healthy life, we have to start from our house.

a) We need to keep the sewerage cum drainage system of the house clean, and we must clean it regularly so that no water will accumulate anywhere within the premises.
b) We must keep the area of the residential building or house free from food waste. All drainage channels should be clean, and insecticide should be sprayed regularly.
c) We must save oil, water, and electricity. We should monitor the consumption of drinking water, electricity, cooking gas, and natural oil.
d) It is necessary to be cautious in using natural resources. In scientific way we have to win over the domestic and industrial smoke and ashes.

e) Society needs to adapt some scientific and lawful system in utilisation of all types of vehicles with private and public vehicles to win over environmental and air pollution.

f) We need to take control of our behaviour and habits before advising others. Because each and every 'I' in society is unitedly become 'we', the human race. When every 'I' is alert, committed, sensible, and reasonable in using our national wealth, then 'we' are strong. Our society, our nation, and the world cannot suffer for our imprudence.

United, we may keep our country pollution-free. A systematic tree plantation process should be made, and that will help stop the erosion of land and spread greenery on earth, with an aim to create clean air.

To get pure drinking water for all, the country requires waste- and dust-free, clean, and healthy air. By maintaining a waste-free society, we may start a good worldwide practice, and at the same time, we may prevent wastage of our national products and natural resources. At every level of our wastage, we are wasting a certain portion of our national resources. We have to keep our work culture eco-friendly and production-friendly. Every degree of per capita loss of man-hours means wastage of national resources and manpower. We have to purify nature and preserve the natural wealth like forests, mineral, and oils.

We may save our nation by reducing loss and wastage of national products. We need to protect and advance our national income and economy in this process.

We have had a successful Clean India programme, by which a nationwide sanitation programme and a cleaning programme have been launched. We have built a comparatively clean India.

Wastage of food grains and all types of consumable merchandise has a vital role in generating pollution. It was not sufficient to bring forth the fantastic success of the Clean India programme, because we could not stop wastage. If wastage is reduced, cleanliness will be better and more effective. Both are correlated. So we need a worthful planned scientific, logical Stop Wastage programme to achieve a pollution-free, healthy nation.

A national task force or social service group consisting of dedicated, energetic, civilised, and active task force members should be prepared, to get a successful healthy body politic. This provision may be commenced at the school level, amongst students, through a common education. It can also be applicable to the senior class level and the preliminary service level. It will create a sense of nationality, moral habits, and a love for nature.

CHAPTER FOUR
A HEALTHY NATION

A STEP TOWARDS A SMART, HEALTHY ZERO-BALANCE NATION

The doctor of the future will give no medicine, but will instruct his patients in cure of the human frame, in diet, and in the cause and prevention of disease.

Thomas Edison

POST-CORONA ECONOMY

I already mentioned in Chapter 1 that COVID-19 has taught us that we are not yet ready to save our men from critical medical hazards.

As per WHO and all published reports since the attack of the coronavirus, it has been found that the mortality rate varies from rural region to rural region, due to geographic positions and natural differences. But it is an established reality that:

a) Boys are more likely than girls to be victims of coronavirus.

Table No. 5

COUNTRY	COVID-19 DEATH TOLL BY SEX (%)							
	TOTAL CASE				TOTAL DEATH			
COUNTRY	AS ON DATE	TOTAL CASE	BOYS %	GIRLS %	AS ON DATE	TOTAL DEATH	BOYS %	GIRLS %
ITALY	08.09.2020	278574	47	53	08.09.2020	35569	57.38	42.62
GERMANY	17.09.2020	265019	50	50	13.09.2020	9345	55.45	44.55
CHAINA	28.02.2020	55924	51	49	28.02.2020	2114	64	36
SPAIN	09.09.2020	538867	46	54	21.05.2020	20518	57	43
BANGLADESH	14.09.2020	339332	71	29	14.09.2020	4759	77	23
SWEDEN	16.09.2020	87345	48	52	15.09.2020	5851	54.66	44.34
INDIA					02.07.2020	17834	68	32

b) Comorbidity of life-threatening diseases existing within people becomes a deciding factor of death from corona.
c) No fixed assessment of death rate by age is possible until or unless the devastating corona infection is stopped. However, the present death toll highlights that boys of up

to ten to fifteen years of age and young adult females are relatively safe so far. People of ages fifteen to twenty-nine are safer than the age group of thirty to seventy-five.

Some data on deaths from the COVID-19 pandemic, sorted by age and from different countries, is given below, in Tables 6 and 7.

Table No. 6

CORONA DEATH BY AGE OF POPULATION			
COUNTRY	Spain as on 22.05.2020	Itali as on 14. 07. 2020	The USA as on 30. 05. 2020
Age group	% of Death	% of Death	% of Death
1 TO 9	0.2	0.2	0.1
10 TO 19	0.3	0	0.1
20 TO 29	0.2	0.1	0.1
30 TO 39	0.3	0.3	0.4
40 TO 49	0.6	0.9	1
50 TO 59	1.5	2.7	2.4
60 TO 69	5.1	10.6	6.7
70 TO 79	14.5	26.1	16.3
80 TO 89	21.2	33.4	28.7
90-	22.2	32.2	

Table No. 7

CORONA DEATH BY AGE OF POPULATION			
New York as on 14.04.2020		India as on 01.07.2020	
Age group	% of Death	Age group	% of Death
0 to 17 year	0.04	1 to 14 year	1
18 to 44 year	4.5	15 to 29 year	3
45 to 64 year	23.1	30 to 44 year	11
65 to 74 year	24.6	45 to 59 year	32
75 + year	47.7	60 to 74 year	39
		75 + year	14

The basic reason of death from COVID-19 is the comparatively poor and weak vital force of a man, and chronic diseases such as cardiac problems, diabetes, liver problems, and cancer.

What we have already learned from the coronavirus pandemic is that the main reason for death from coronavirus is weakness in physical fitness and a weak vital force. Those who already have lost capacity to fight against the virus.

We need to be health-conscious and attentive to each other and keep our society clean and clear of pollution to get enough fresh and healthy air. We need to be well prepared to face any further attack of corona or other more fatal viruses.

Towards the Dream of a Zero-Balance Health Programme

A Caring Society Benefits Us All

It is a shame to say that due to less immunisation and poor health conditions, girls are mostly unable to fight physically and mentally against ill treatment worldwide, and they become the easiest targets of social and domestic violence.

Here I have highlighted some recent health-related data that are annually published by international organisations like ILO, WHO, OECD, the World Bank, and so on, which depict the weak health structures of the countries in this world.

Like education, we need to go on a health programme at the beginning of a child's birth. Every year in India as well as in the world countries we face child death during and after parturition.

Table No. 8

	GLOBAL MORTALITY RATE AND MEDICAL FACILITIES AVAILABLE													
	Child below 5 yr. PER 1000		Live birth mother PER 100000		Maleria Per–1000		Tuberculisis Per100000		HIV Per–1000		No. of Patient per Doctor & Nurse	
REGION	2000	2018	2000	2017	2000	2018	2000	2018	2000	2018	Doctor	Nurse
AFRICA	152	76	857	525	365	229	329	231	3.14	1.07	3324	985
AMERICA	26	14	73	57	14	7	36	29	0.23	0.16	417	120
SOUTH EAST ASIA	84	34	355	152	19	5	299	220	0.27	0.09	1239	559
EUROPE	21	8	22	13	1	0	52	28	0.12	0.19	293	123
EAST MEDITARINIAN	82	47	330	164	20	10	128	115	0.03	0.07	989	690
WESTERN PECIFC	35	12	75	41	4	3	135	96	0.08	0.06	533	275

	HEALTH AND MEDICAL FACILITIES PER 1000							MORTALITY RATE PER 100,000				
	DOCTOR PER 1000 PATIENT				NURSE & MID WIES PER 1000			MATERNAL LIFE BIRTH		POLLUTION		
COUNTRIES	2000-01	2005	2010	2017-18	2000	2005	2010	2017-18	2010	2017	2000	2006	2016
CUBA	5.93	6.27	6.81	8.42	7.49	NA	9.17	7.56	41	36	49.5	58	42
GEORGIA	3.83	3.38	4.44	7.12	4.7	4.14	3.95	4.73	32	25	101.8	140	73
LITHUANIA	3.29	3.3	4.3	6.35	8.01	7.55	7.59	9.84	10	8	34	51	23
GREECE	4.26	3.38	3.94	5.48	2.88	3.49	3.76	3.63	3	3	28	36	20
CHAINA	1.23	1.21	1.45	1.98	0.97	1	1.48	2.66	36	29	112.7	126	100
PAKISTHAN	0.64	0.79	0.8	0.98	0.42	NA	0.56	0.66	191	140	174	197	149
INDIA	0.52	0.57	0.66	0.73	1.16	1.29	0.87	1.72	210	145	184	202	166
BANGLADESH	0.25	0.31	0.36	0.58	0.42	0.28	0.18	0.41	258	173	149	161	137

POST-CORONA ECONOMY

In Table 8 and its associated charts (8a to 8g) below, we can find data on mortality rates and some health facilities available for the masses. It is to bring forth the burning issues before society, to be considered with the highest priority for the benefit of society.

Chart 8a

Mortality of Child below 5 yr.- per 1000 by Region

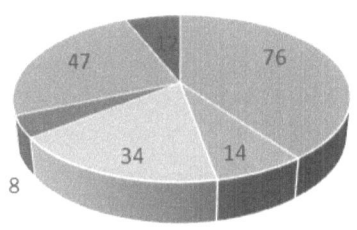

- AFRICA
- AMERICA
- SOUTH EAST ASIA
- EUROPE
- EAST MEDITARINIAN
- WESTERN PECIFIC

Chart 8b

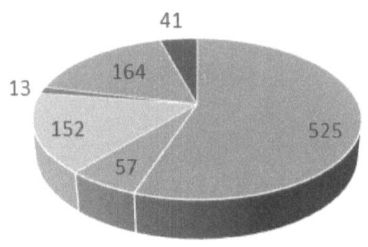

Mortality Live birth mother PER 100000 by Region

- AFRICA
- AMERICA
- SOUTH EAST ASIA
- EUROPE
- EAST MEDITARINIAN
- WESTERN PECIFIC

Chart 8c

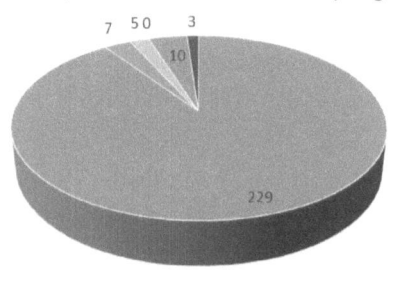

Mortality from Maleria Per-1000 by Region

- AFRICA
- AMERICA
- SOUTH EAST ASIA
- EUROPE
- EAST MEDITARINIAN
- WESTERN PECIFIC

POST-CORONA ECONOMY

Chart 8d

Mortality fromTuberculosis-Per 100000

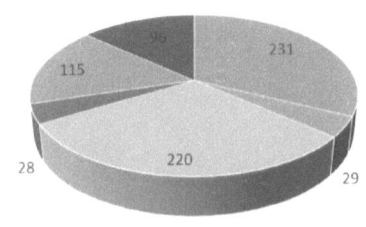

- AFRICA
- AMERICA
- SOUTH EAST ASIA
- EUROPE
- EAST MEDITARINIAN
- WESTERN PECIFIC

Chart 8e

Mortality from HIV Per- 1000 by Region

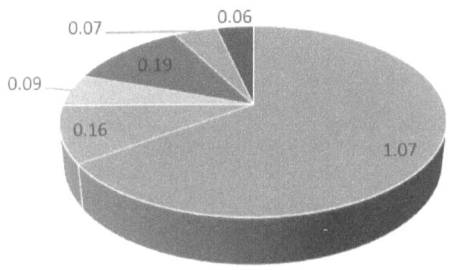

- AFRICA
- AMERICA
- SOUTH EAST ASIA
- EUROPE
- EAST MEDITARINIAN
- WESTERN PECIFIC

Chart 8f

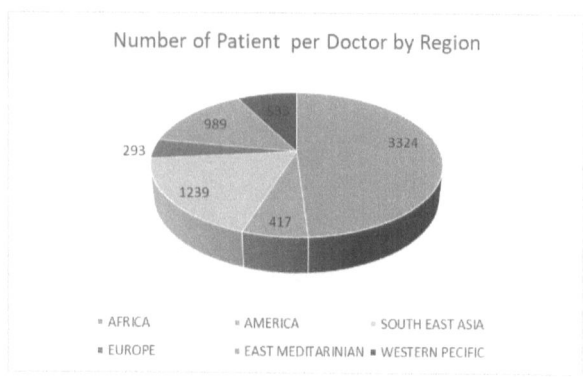

Chart 8g

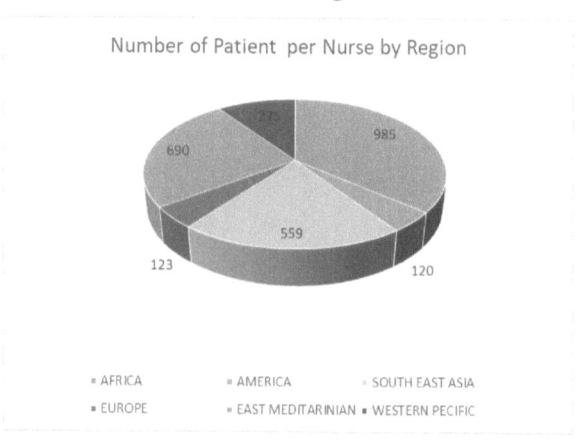

Whether we admit it or not, our world needs to give more attention to the health sector. The death rates of live-birth mothers and children below five years significantly throw light on requirement of a major attention and prequestionnaire measure on national health programmes. Africa, South East Asia, and East Mediterranean regions are relatively far behind in progress. Even the responsibility of patient per doctor, nurse, and midwife are very high. That signifies the need of sufficient medical team to strengthen the health sector. But some developing nations do not have enough infrastructure and economic ability to challenge it unless the countries take a positive way to resolve the problem.

A Healthy Baby Is a Healthy Man and a Healthy Nation

It is the main point: Sufficient progress in health sector is must to be marked as a healthy nation. There is a proverb that says, 'A stitch in time saves nine.' It is the same consequence for human life. If we can raise a healthy kid, we can ensure a healthy citizen and a healthy society in the long run. If immunity is strong in childhood, it helps a man or woman be healthy throughout their life. At the same time, a healthy child will no doubt require proportionately less health support throughout life. On the other hand, a weak and unhealthy child will create a weak and unhealthy society, and will always require health support to make it through by any means.

Regrettably, we all are making mistake in our own home. The primary source of the population is badly handled in our society. Yes, it is the girl child, the future mother, and the creator of society.

From birth, a girl child should be treated in a healthy direction and provided with sufficient medical backing and exceptional attention to nurture the immunisation power within them. Only then will they be able to give birth to a healthy child.

In modern society also, the total mortality rate is very high worldwide, due to poor health, malnutrition, viral and contaminating diseases (cholera, the plague, typhoid, pox, etc.), and non-communicable diseases (NCD), like diabetes, heart disease, liver problems, etc. At the same time, the morbidity rate of pregnant women and children, newborns up to five years of age, is very high in many countries in the world, including India and our neighbouring states. Today the death rate of pregnant women and newborn children in hospital beds is really alarming. Even after birth, up to five years of age, children die of malnutrition and unhealthy living.

To build up a healthy nation, it is required to spread national health programmes and establish health centre cum hospital at every corner or rural and urban areas of the country, which is expensive. To stop a huge expenditure for the medical platform, it is better that we take steps during the prevention stage, the early stage of childhood.

Hence, we need a complete system to spread healthcare to everyone. No question, it will also cut the overall medical expenditure of a country and reduce the morbidity rate of untimely death, and at the same time, the country will get a healthy body politic.

Providing health for all is not a tough job at all. It is not a matter of high expenditure also. It could be achieved easily. It only requires remodelling of the existing house and state-wide health system and constitution. It is required to distribute wisely to every corner of the society, whether rural or urban.

It is true that the national health programmes for childhood immunisation are provided regularly by governments. However, it does not reach every last baby or child. We need to cater to every child within a process and schema.

The All-Purpose National Citizen Life Card

One nation, one citizen, one card. A common all-purpose digital national citizen life card, which may be digitally controlled in a centralised system is required in place of all existing identity cards like voter card, ration card, Health-card, citizenship card, etc. The card can easily be the controlling device of a nation. It will be a single identity card for one citizen from the cradle to the grave. No other identity card is needed for a citizen. The card, digitally printed and coded with a nationalised serial number, will be issued to a newborn baby during his or her birth. It will digitally record the baby's health, birth, and parental history. Through this card, the parents will avail baby health programme facilities at every corner of the country either free of cost or with payment. It will only need identity card to get admission. The card will have the function of a ration card, all-purpose life health card, income tax cum PAN card, voter identity card, and many others. The card will be the only acceptable identity card for entrance fees; registration at schools, colleges, organisations, universities, or any educational institutes; and hospitals and health centres within the local area or abroad. The card should be surrendered at the time of death.

The same citizen life card is to be provided to all citizens of a nation in the same line, purpose, and procedure, with the same common benefit to the existing citizen. Therefore, the entire national population will come under a single plan and system under a centralised data bank.

The identity card will be digitally controlled, monitored, and centralised from the birth of a baby and of all citizen. A complete up-to-date history and data on health, education, service, and all of population will be one click away. The data will automatically reveal the health as well as the physical and financial status of the citizen or population. The ready response team and the regional social service group member will provide necessary assistance. The citizen data bank will automatically provide up-to-date data to analyse national growth, wellness, education, income, service, population, child health, morbidity rate, and so on. The data will slash the spending of many national health and census programmes. When the card is used for national electoral programmes, unnecessary expenditures in elections will be lessened.

National child health card: During the discharge of a newborn baby from the hospital, along with the birth certificate, the parent of the infant will be provided a national citizen life card. The same will be used as a national child health card, with parental and birth stories. The card will be utilised for the purpose of the national post birth baby health surveillance system of the country. It will be used for very controlled, systematic compulsory post birth vaccination, immunisation, and the national health assistance plan and handling, along with a birth certificate, by which the parents will get complimentary or paid treatment from any government health centre.

1) **Child health monitoring**: Through the national child health card cum national citizen health card, all preschool children will get full health and medical support, either at home or at the nearest government health centre, free of cost in every corner of the country, whether rural or urban. Where a required number of health centre is not available, local national public service offices like panchayat offices, corporation office buildings, local clubhouse buildings, or NGO office buildings will be utilised for the successful arrangement of all common national health programmes, to get rid of malnutrition, immunisation deficiency, and other post birth health problems in children.
2) **Total immunisation programme**: All national health programmes in the country should be monitored by a national centralised system linked to the *national citizen life card* provided to the children and to all citizens, so there will

be no possibility of children being left out of immunisation programmes.

3) **A health programme at the school level:** Every primary school, secondary school, and higher secondary school should have a medical room cum doctors' chamber, with a *doctor cum health adviser* and nursing assistant permanently appointed. They will go along with the second form of the health check-up programme linked with the provided national citizen health card. In this way, the normal health programme will be handed over to the doctor after school from pre-primary to secondary and higher secondary stages.

4) **Health education:** In pre-primary and primary schools, the doctor cum health adviser, as a routine job other than regular health check-ups and medication at school, may also teach a health class to instruct the students how to keep fit, and the adviser may aid in building basic health habits and health knowledge. The health adviser, from time to time, should inform and advise the guardians of the children on their health progress and health-related deficiencies, for recovery.

5) **Health education and adolescent:** In upper primary to middle and higher secondary levels, i.e. up to the twelfth class level, the doctors will find out the common health problem of the students and do regular check-ups and also take classes in advanced health education and provide basic

knowledge on adolescent and its physical and health consciousness to produce a healthy student.

6) **Healthy mother, healthy baby:** The girl students, in this period, will be specially protected and their physical fitness medically cared for, due to their ongoing hormonal development and the conversion period of pubescence. In this way, we can easily minimise and prevent the morbidity and mortality rate of pregnant women and reduce mortality rates during child birth. It will also reduce neonatal problems and death at a very young age. In this way, we can assure the zero-balance immunisation system of the children and the perfect health system, generating a win–win situation of healthy mother and healthy baby that will gift us a healthy country.

7) **Health and sports:** Sports is another very important and compulsory source of physical fitness for a child. The sports teacher, with the cooperation of the doctor, will monitor and improve the fitness of the pupils. They will provide proper lessons and training and advice on sports suitable for the individual pupils.

The perfect performance of health programmes will be marked and monitored through the national citizen life card at the school layer. Every birth, immunisation in childhood, and health control will be systematically monitored without failure.

The medical system, without any extra outlay for the census on the growth of population, education and national health status, morbidity rate, and henceforth, will help get a national health data bank automatically in the system.

Hence, up to higher secondary (i.e. precollege) levels or up to the ages of fifteen to sixteen, the total health system is to be controlled and monitored by the national health system. It could be free of cost for up to a certain grade level, like Class VIII or Class X level, and for the remaining period, i.e. from Class IX or XI to XII or more, there will be a monthly or yearly fee. The total health monitoring system will ensure a healthy boy or girl—a healthy citizen in the long run. The healthy lifestyle will end and reduce malnutrition in childhood, and the morbidity rate will reduce to a very negligible rate or to zero units. Moreover, the rest of a person's life will be very healthy. This remaining living period may require comparatively minimal medical and wellness support for a citizen, and automatically, the national medical expenditure of the state will be lessened.

The entire student life of every child will be under the control of a health management organisation with education on ideal health management. The students will also be trained with system and procedure in pollution control, protection and pollution reducing management. For the total duration of school education, the doctor cum health adviser and the nursing and health assistant appointed in the school will be the only representatives for the task. So, the doctor will be appointed based on the proportion of total student of the school, or it could be arranged from doctors' platforms on a hire basis.

The doctors cum health advisers could also be trainee doctors from medical colleges, for their in-house training period after receiving their medical degrees.

In case of any critical problem, the students will be referred to the local health centre or hospital as per recommendation of the doctor. All the existing students should be taken into account under the same health programme provided through the national citizen life card.

At pre-school period, through a centralised and digitalised system, the child-health management programmes could be provided with grand success at Public health centres, a mobile health service system. At school level heath check-up and treatment, health education, advice, control and follow-up will be provided by appointed doctor cum-health instructor and health-assistant. In this process, the total wellness maintenance of children will provide a successful immunised healthy society. Thus, the aspiration of a complete zero-balance healthy body politic will be determined.

CHAPTER FIVE

A SMART NATION

THE MISSION OF A ZERO-BALANCE EDUCATED SOCIETY

> Knowledge is power. Information is liberating. Education is the premise of progress, in every society, in every family.
>
> **Kofi Annan**

Towards the Dream of a Zero-Balance Education

Complete Literacy

Today each country is trying to spread education to the grassroots level, to educate people from childhood. But unfortunately, it is still a long way before it can be achieved.

Table No. 9

WORLD LITERICY STATUS OF PEOPLE OF AGE 15 YEARS AND ABOVE COMPARED WITH TOTAL POPULATION OF WORLD BY REGION											
	TOTAL POPUPATION REGION WISE IN THE YEAR 2018			LITERACY STATUS DURING 2000 TO 2018 (18 YEARS)								
				BOTH SEX			MALE			FEMALE		
REGIONS	IN 2018	MALE	FEMALE	2000	2010	2018	2000	2010	2018	2000	2010	2018
World	7.592 BILLION	3.826 BILLION	3.763 BILLION	80.779	84.040	86.301	89.846	91.835	92.867	75.446	79.883	82.768
South Asia	1.814 BILLION	396914659	377474085	57.689	66.019	72.252	80.184	86.705	91.121	44.930	55.527	63.729
North America	363809186	180028719	183716548	NA	NA	NA	NA	NA	NA	NA	NA	NA
Middle East & North Africa	448912962	232514589	216398372	NA	NA	NA	NA	NA	NA	NA	NA	NA
Latin America & Caribean	640454810	314959140	325640259	89.032	91.667	93.867	94.557	97.033	98.355	88.203	91.110	93.448
Europe & Central Asia	917922618.5	443797581	471919784	96.583	97.581	98.340	99.285	99.560	99.684	95.353	96.819	97.882
East Asia & Pacific	2.328 BILLION	1.18 BILLION	1.148 BILLION	90.314	94.268	95.608	94.557	98.719	98.669	86.325	92.023	93.940
Sub Saharan Africa	1.078 BILLION	537932967	540373553	56.660	59.564	65.577	72.917	75.413	79.455	47.407	51.045	58.801

In Table 9, I have tried to highlight the educational level of people above fifteen years of age around the world, by region. Fact is compared to the total world population in the year 2018. This information leads us to the following conclusions and reflections.

Table No. 10

A comperative study on Region wise literacy progress rate of 15years and above age people by Total, Annual and by sex during the year 2000 to 2018

Region	Literacy Progress during 2000-2018 and rank in %					Male : Female progress status in %					
	Total in 2018	Rank	Total 18 yr	Total Annual	Rank		Total Male	Male Annual		Total Female	Female Annual	Rank
World	86.301		5.522	0.30%			3.021	0.17%	Back	7.322	0.41%	Advance
South Asia	72.252	4th	14.563	0.81%	1st		10.937	0.607	Back	18.799	1.044	Advance
Latin America & Caribbean	93.867	3rd	4.835	0.268	4th		3.798	0.211	Back	5.245	0.291	Advance
Europe & Central Asia	98.334	1st	1.757	0.097	5th		0.399	0.022	Back	2.529	0.14	Advance
East Asia & Pacific	95.608	2nd	5.294	0.294	3rd		0.399	0.022	Back	7.615	0.423	Advance
Sub Saharan Africa	65.577	5th	8.917	0.495	2nd		6.538	0.363	Back	11.394	0.633	Advance

Observations:

a) Out of seven regions, no data is available on (1) North America and (2) the Middle East and North Africa.
b) During this time, in overall literacy, Europe and Central Asia are leading at first place. East Asia and Pacific stand at second, and Latin America and Caribbean, South Asia, and sub-Saharan Africa stand at third, fourth, and fifth place, respectively.
c) In terms of actual annual literacy progress by region, South Asia stands at first place, with its total progress from 2000 to 2018 at 14.563% and annual progress at 0.81%. Sub-Saharan Africa, which has the lowest total literacy rate, now marches towards second place, with an annual progress of 0.495%. East Asia and Pacific, Latin America and Caribbean, and Europe and Central Asia hold third, fourth, and fifth place respectively, having an annual progress rate of 0.294%, 0.268%, and 0.097%, respectively.
d) Hopefully and remarkably, girls, who have been completely inhibited by all means in society throughout the decades, are marching forward with more grace than boys in all parts. While the annual literacy progress of boys ranges from 0.022% to 0.607% in those regions, girls' annual literacy progress rate ranges from 0.14% to 1.044%.

Only an educated society can provide powerful and expert manpower and quality output. But education starts at nursery age. So nursery and primary education up to secondary level training should be given to each kid, to get absolute literacy in the state. There is no other alternative to complete literacy. Otherwise, progress in literacy is quite impossible.

Table No. 11

STATUS OF DROP OUT FROM SCHOOL OF CHILDREN AT PRIMARY SCHOOL LEVEL BY WORLD BANK INCOME GROUP CUMULATIVE DROP OUT RATE AT PRIMARY SCHOOL LEVEL

ASSESMENT BY	BOTH SEX (%)					BOYS (%)					GIRLS (%)				
	2013	2014	2015	2016	2017	2013	2014	2015	2016	2017	2013	2014	2015	2016	2017
World Bank Income															
Low income countries	50.09	49.27	48.73	48.58	48.60	51.90	51.90	51.30	51.10	51.10	48.10	46.40	45.90	45.80	45.90
Lower middle-income	21.55	16.34	16.81	18.11	15.74	22.10	17.20	17.80	18.40	16.70	21.00	15.40	15.70	17.80	14.70
Middle income countries	20.49	13.96	13.90	14.18	12.77	21.10	14.60	14.80	14.60	13.60	19.80	13.20	12.90	13.80	11.80
Upper middle-income	18.66	9.80	8.84	7.59	7.81	19.42	10.20	9.47	8.05	8.46	17.83	9.35	8.15	7.07	7.10
High income countries	5.33	5.26	5.42	4.87	4.48	5.46	5.41	5.56	5.01	4.63	5.20	5.11	5.28	4.72	4.32

Table No. 12

STATUS OF PRE-PRIMARY (NURSURY), PRIMARY, & TARTIARY EDUCATION BY REGION

REGION	A) OUT OF SCHOOL IN MILLION			B) REGIONAL PRE PRIMARY EDUCATION GAP BY								C) TERTIARY EDUCATION BY PERSENTAGE (%)			
				BY SEX		ATTENDANCE		BY LOCATION		BY WEALTH					
	2005	2010	2014	BOYS	GIRLS	BOYS	GIRLS	URBAN	RURAL	RICH	POOR	2000	2005	2010	2014
South Asia	18.34	13.03	11.32	26	24	82	81	87	79	94	68	8.21	9.45	15.86	20.84
North America	1.23	1.30	1.48	72	73	NA	NA	NA	NA	NA	NA	67.24	79.88	90.81	84.03
Middle East & North Africa	2.70	1.62	2.19	31	31	51	51	55	47	59	43	19.90	23.20	30.42	36.42
Latin America & Carabean	2.79	2.49	3.48	78	79	95	95	96	93	98	92	21.95	27.96	39.42	43.30
Europe & Central Asia	1.16	1.00	1.11	76	75	NA	NA	NA	NA	NA	NA	38.80	51.37	58.00	62.07
East Asia & Pacific	9.10	6.38	6.30	82	83	89	90	91	88	93	82	11.49	19.90	24.75	36.47
West and Central Africa	37.85	35.52	34.13	30	31	53	52	71	44	80	29	1.41	6.07	7.86	8.59
Eastern and Southern				37	36	66	66	83	60	88	49				

A) out of school children at primary education age im million; B) Regional gap in Pre Primary education by sex, by attendance,by location and by wealth and C) Region wise Tertiary education rate worldwide.

(Data collected from UNICEF Global Data 2019, UNICEF Institute for Statistics, World Database, World Bank Data.)

Education is yet to reach a portion of people in society. The nation needs to educate each and every family in society. Teaching has to reach all the masses.

Here I have tried to share some information along with the global education scenario on child education from nursery to tertiary education. Particular emphasis was given to the pre-primary to primary and junior class students of the age groups below five years to fifteen years.

Tables 11 and 12 highlight the global picture of literacy, from pre-primary to tertiary education, in different world regions.

The data reveals that in 2017, the dropout rate from school in the primary education level is higher in low-income countries. Whilst the dropout rate in the high-income group is just 4.48%, the upper-middle-income countries are at 7.81%, the middle-income group is at 12.71%, the lower-middle-income group is at 15.75%, and the low-income group's dropout rate is at 48.60%. It is only a 2% decrease in five years, compared to its rate of 50.09% in 2013, in the low-income group; whilst it is far better in the lower-middle, middle, and upper-middle groups respectively, with rates of 21.55%, 20.49%, and 18.66% in 2013. The dropout rates at the elementary school level for boys and girls are the same from 2013 to 2017. Exceptionally, in high-income countries, the decline of dropout cases is very minimal; it is less than 1% in five years. It was 5.33% in 2013 and 4.48% in 2017.

The conclusion is that the financial factor works as the main roadblock to growth at pre-primary and elementary levels in low-income groups, whilst the dropout cases in rich families are wilful and voluntary.

In the case of development in child education, there is a very minimal difference in the ratio of sex. The present system has established the priority of training for both boys and girls from nursery to higher education. But the gender ratio and all education facilities vary from region to region due to local infrastructural barriers and communication systems highly influenced by economic discrimination in the state. In sub-Saharan Africa, 34.13 million boys and girls in 2014 could not have education. The gross enrolment ratio for nursery or pre-primary education was boys 37:31 in West and Central Africa and 37:36 of Eastern and Southern Africa. The net attendance in pre-primary students' ratio of boys and girls in West and Central Africa is 53:52 and in Eastern and Southern Africa it is 66:66. The education gap between boys and girls in urban and rural areas of the same regions are respectively 71:44 and 83:60. The economic hardship is another hindrance in nursery and primary education; it varies too much in ratio between richest and poorest. The nursery education ratio in boys and girls in South Asia – 94:68, Middle East and North Africa – 59:43, Latin America and Caribbean – 98:92, East Asia and Pacific – 93:82, and in West and Central Africa, Eastern and Southern Africa it is respectively 80:29 and 88:49.

Compared to the scenario in sub-Saharan Africa, the child education scenario is far better in other regions.

However, the out-of-school rate in other regions is still far more serious. In 2014, it was 11.32 million in South Asia, 1.48 million in North America, 2.19 million in Middle East and North Africa, 3.48 million in Latin America and Caribbean, 1.11 million in Europe and Central Asia, and 6.30 million in East Asia and Pacific.

The variations in ratio in education from nursery level to higher levels are all but the same picture in all other neighbourhoods also. It is observed, that the boys and girls gender ratio vary very slightly in education. But the local natural atmosphere and the infrastructural barriers in urban and rural areas to attend school is a matter of concern. We may also concentrate on financial discrimination in citizens, which is another obstruction in educational progress. Overall, we have to realise that, the global literacy growth is below 0.5%.

Education for those above fifteen to twenty-four years of age is also not remarkable, despite attempts being made by the countries. There was about 4–6% growth in four years in all areas of the world, except sub-Saharan Africa, which sustained only 1% growth in four years, from 2010 to 2014.

From this, we can conclude that the region, location, and natural obstacles and discrimination in economic capacity are the prime barriers to total education. It has to be solved before we can get to the goal. Distribution of healthy mid-day meal in schools is a great attempt, but until or unless the family economic structure is ensured, dropouts and low attendance in nursery as well as out-of-school youths at primary school age may not be terminated. Unless the education system reaches even the remote areas, even at the doorstep of a society with health security, the dream of zero-balance education is impossible.

The answer is no. Today each developed and developing country is trying its best to wipe out illiteracy. Nevertheless, it is sure that money is the primary cause behind poor literacy.

It is the scarcity of money in the hands of poor households. When even one piece of bread is not regularly available to some households, how can we expect a family to permit the kids to travel to school? Both father and mother are out of the house to search for daily rations. Do we expect the child to arrive at school alone when his or her parent is out?

Thus, in most cases, the boys and girls learn to take an active role in the struggle of the existence of the ménage. Therefore, the alphabet characters *A*, *B*, and *C*, to those poor children, stand for *alms*, *bread*, and *cooking*, because it is the life in front of the innocent children.

Every family first needs some financial power in hand to spare for the child to attend class. The poor families cannot earn enough money to maintain family, so money should have to pass to the poor by way of wages to strengthen the societal structure. Only then will all families be mentally convinced and prepared to send their children to school.

Then comes the question of education. Supplying food or midday meals to the children in school is a noble effort to bring the pupil in the school. But are we truly succeeding in this mission? Why are we not able to make everyone literate? Midday meals and free books for the children have not been able to bring absolute success to this noble mission.

Who then is responsible for the failure? Are the parents of the kids responsible for this, or is it the schoolhouse?

In progressive modern society, some parents feel that a girl child does not require education; only the boy child will go to school. Is it a drama or a reality show? Do the parents think so for their innocent girl child?

I can boldly say that it is not a truthful affirmation. We can recite two lines from 'Debotar Grash', by our great poet Rabindranath Tagore: 'Oh god, you have only listened to the words that came out from the mouth! Could you not attend to the voice that came out from the core of the heart of a mother?' ('Shudhu ki mukher Katha shunecho devata? Shononi ki jananir antarer Katha?')

Yes, it is the actual truth. It is, in reality, a great sacrifice of a parent. In case of insufficient funds to live, it is better to at least raise the boy child with education and health so that, in turn, he can lead a family. Meanwhile, the girl child is not only excluded from education, but in some cases, she is given insufficient food as well. It is with the consolation in mind that she will be given a marriage with a good groom.

But originally in present society, the illiterate one also wants both son and daughter to be provided good and proper education so that she can win over the challenges of her odd days in future life. It is only because of poverty and shortage of work that sometimes the poor family is bound to make the unfortunate and adverse decision. If they had money, they would try to give sufficient education to all their children.

Again, it is the poor financial capacity that makes poor families bound to stop education. So education should reach the poor at the base point, at their doorstep.

The education system should have to give highest priority. Attempt to be made to spread education at every corner of the society. It should be at every corner of the cities and villages, rural and urban areas even under the thatched house of the farmers and workers beside the paddy field and workshops. It is essential to ease out the anxiety over the future of little ones of the farmers and workers. When a single one child irrespective of sex and cast will not be left out from education, only then we can dream of a zero-balance education is achieved.

The poor parents, as well as the children, will have to be convinced that the only thing besides food that can make their life better is education.

We should leave no stone unturned to achieve the success over the mission of complete literacy. It is only success when the last child of the society is educated. When the last child can smile with an expression of satisfaction and happiness, then the mission and dream of a zero-balance learned society may be made.

We are already, in that way, advanced. Our children now get free education, and they receive free reading materials. They get free midday meals in school.

At present, we have to take a few more steps forward. We have to make a system of education for all, for the left-out children from preparatory to junior high level, i.e. Class VII. Education will not be limited to school premises. It will be spread everywhere, from urban to rural areas, at every corner of the country.

No, it will not take a very heavy fiscal burden. We can easily spread education through the surviving social organisations of local government bodies, like the panchayat office buildings, clubhouse buildings, etc. Even in the rural areas beside the farmers' land, under a temporary shed, and in open air also. I believe, we are blessed with the great souls within us in our country, who will value mission and aggressively come forward to make it grand success. We also have CSR funds to support the mission for a short time.

In this way, we can educate the left-out children from pre-nursery to junior high class, i.e. Class VII.

Each and every child will be enrolled for education under the same digitally controlled Citizen health card from the beginning of schooling. The education along with health will be monitored and controlled successively to stop early dropout from school and health factors.

Each and every school must obtain at least one doctor and a nurse with a chamber, depending on the number of students, to monitor the health of the students at school daily and to provide proper health education to the kids from the beginning so that a healthy society can rise up automatically. By commission of wellness education and supplying of all necessary childcare, vaccines, and injections at school, free of cost through child healthcare programmes, the immunity of the children will increase.

We need to proceed with another health mission for the children in school. It is *weightless education*. COVID-19 has made us leap to studying from home. It is one form of digital education. Digital education is possible for the upper class, but the pre-primary and primary students need fundamentally book-based teaching.

Double set of books: we can take a target of weightless education for the children for their health security. Two sets of hard-copy of books or one hard-copy and one digital copy or both digital copies can solve the weightless education target. One set either hard-copy or digital will be used at classroom and the second one will be at house for further preparation of lessons at home. One hard-copy set of books at school is for a regular course of study. It could be a digital book also, like a digital blackboard or digital desk, and other hard-copy books set for preparation of studying at home.

It can provide weightless health education for our children up to Madhyamika standard, with a few additions and alterations as per the need of the higher grade. A very minimal number of copybooks is also needed for the lesson. Only one diary cum instruction notebook as triangle communication media among teacher-student-parents is to be maintained throughout the session for instruction and monitoring of education. Semester wise, one or two multi-subject copy of book for class and homework will only carry the student along with pen, pencil, etc.

No, it is not the five kilograms or more of reading material to be carried on the small shoulders of kids. The maximum weight to be supported by the students, as per routine, is a maximum of 500 grams to 1 kilogram. But it will assist in reducing physical problems and fear of an overweight school bag.

Furthermore, to see the total literacy of the country, the same healthcare card offered during the birth of a child will be the tracking instrument of the education of the student in the same national centralised monitoring system. The same identification number (ID no.) and the card will be the admission instrument for the entire lifespan of the citizen.

All existing students admitted in private and public schools all over the country will also be enrolled in the same system. Each and every student of the country be covered under the same common facilities with the same Citizen health card with personalised identification number.

In this way, each and every child and all existing students will come under a single platform and the same tracking system. The benefit is that each and every student from pre-primary to higher levels will be provided the same health education and medical facilities during their school life; hence, the prolonged threat of poor health and malnutrition of the babies will come under control. It will give us a healthy-baby society. It will also ensure proper and complete education of the children in the country.

It will also stop students from dropping and leaving school at an early age, for in the process, all students in any class will remain under the surveillance of a centralised monitoring system, including their health and medication through the medical facility at the school layer. The dropout students will automatically be identified and tracked down to be made to return to school at the local education centre nearest their house, if needed.

Moreover, the education system should be positive, as well as creative, to build up an efficient workforce to improve the nation. After completion of secondary education, there should be one year of compulsory technical and basic training programmes for boys and girls in the same school, as part of the education completed at the secondary level. The boys and girls will need basic training in teaching, nursing, and agriculture, as well as various technical and non-technical courses, with short-term practical experience so that they can actively take part in domestic demand as well as fulfil a social need. The same one-year training experience will help in making a decision in post-secondary education.

In this fashion, the dream of a *completely literate and healthy nation* will be successfully accomplished.

CHAPTER SIX
EVERY MAN HAS HIS WORK

A DREAM OF A NATION WITH ZERO-BALANCE EMPLOYMENT

Unemployment is bigger than a political party. It is a national danger and a national scandal.
Ellen Wilkinson

New markets could be created by rural potentials, which could lead to rise in the employment.
A. P. J. Abdul Kalam

POST-CORONA ECONOMY

Unemployment is no doubt a curse to society. Unemployment rates are increasing day by day. Coronavirus has suddenly raised the worldwide unemployment total manyfold. The destructive influence of the coronavirus is so far from over. An unnatural fear of dying has increased in human minds worldwide.

The national economy, as well as the world economy, is being threatened. Every state is now fighting tooth and nail against the destructive and deadly coronavirus. Now almost all world countries are facing the challenge to keep control over death from Corona Pandemic.

I will later present charts that highlight the present morbidity rates and the rates of unemployment and business closures of different countries, as well as of the world.

Our physicians, nurses, and all the health workers in India and the world countries are dedicatedly and breathlessly fighting to save lives from the clutches of the pandemic. World organisations, world leaders, and great scientists are all dedicatedly engaged in discovering and inventing a weapon, i.e. a medicine, to defeat the corona pandemic.

A small virus has given the world a deadly lesson to learn, and has thrown the world before a challenge to survive the ongoing pandemic. COVID-19 has practically sent us an open message to be prepared physically, mentally, medically, and economically, to fight against upcoming new versions of viruses, pandemics, and so on.

All of a sudden, we realise our jobs have vanished. We are trying to get rid of the onset of an invisible enemy called a virus. Economic growth is now running poorly. Medical, health, and education systems have been interrupted. The unemployment rate is climbing quickly. Millions of workers have lost their jobs. As per world estimates, ILO has already predicted that about 5 million to 25 million workers around the world will lose their jobs.

Production homes are closed. Workers are not receiving their wages. All types of shops, transportation, rails, and flights are completely shut down. It is a total massacre of economic growth. Globally, almost all types of investment is stopped due to fund crisis caused by suspension of production, work, and non-availability of consumers, closures in business houses, etc. Small-scale industries are suffering from fund and labour shortages. Large-scale production houses have stopped production due to the corona pandemic, and daily workers and a percentage of permanent workers have been forced out by their employers.

A lot of workers have voluntarily left their companies to return to their villages. Employment from home has taken place in digitalised companies to maintain the essential work. Millions in the migrant daily labour force, including their family members, have lost their jobs, roofs, and food. Therefore, as panic struck and fear of the pandemic overpowered the migrant workers, a large number of the migrant workers have left voluntarily for their house at remote distance. Due to non-availability of transport, they have set out on foot to reach their house at long distance.

It's now like a traumatic experience for the workers. The entire national economy is troubled. Millions and millions of dollars have been spent to win over COVID-19, but in vain. The destruction rate is still rising day by day. Corona has proven that we are not powerful enough to fight against it. We have weapons worth millions of dollars for the army, but no small weapons for our great soldiers, the doctors, so that they can fight against corona, a very small but deadly virus. The sole weapon is a therapeutic and prophylactic medicine to kill corona; it is the only key to stopping COVID-19 and winning over death.

Nowadays we are facing the challenge of resurrecting the down sliding national economy. Nature has penalised the world for recklessness over consumption and wastage of natural wealth. We have to make up for it and regain our power in every sphere of life.

The world is suffering from low immunity and malnutrition. To get the upper hand over the coronavirus and other upcoming viruses, we have to wipe out malnutrition and develop high immunity amongst all from childbirth. We have to fight off the contamination problem and save nature with the proper pollution-control system, as discussed in the pollution chapter.

But what about the way to raise the down sliding economy?

Printing money is not a solution. Donations, assistance, etc. are not a durable solution. The only solution lies in a renaissance in production, consumption, and building up a wide range of consumers whilst minimising the wastage in production and raw materials and natural resources. As per the FAO Annual Report 2014, we are facing wastage of one-third of the annual production of food products and more. That, considering all social, natural, physical, and metaphysical types of wastage in price value and cost, is more than 2.6 trillion US dollars. It is based on food products alone. When all types of consumables are considered, it could go over 4 trillion US dollars.

We have to stop the wastage through proper care and protection, and we have to remove all the barriers to progress. We can strengthen national income and save money if we can bell the cat. We have to generate consumers and increase production, so we need money in every hand. Unless we build up the consumption power, the utility will not be raised, and consumption is then nothing but a dream.

Taking all this into consideration, we need money, i.e. consumption power, in all hands. We have to create and spread jobs, save money, and spread money to every hand, rather than to a few men. The new consumers will drive up production.

Table No. 13

REGION WISE AVERAGE UNEMPLOYMENT (%)					
REGION WITH TOTAL COUNTRY	HIGHEST AND LOWEST UNEMPLOYMENT OF REGION				
NAME	%	COUNTRY	%	COUNTRY	%
WORLD (182 COUNTRIES)		7.04 SOUTH AFRICA	28..18	QATER	0.09
UROPEAN UNION (26 COUNTRIES)		6.03 GREECE	17.24	CZECH REP	1.93
EUROPE (42 COUNTRIES)		7.04 BOSNIA & HERZ	18.42	CZECH REP	1.93
ASIA (46 COUNTRIES)		5.73 PALESTINE	26.17	QATER	0.09
AFRICA (52 COUNTRIES)		8.18 SOUTH AFRICA	28.18	NIGER	0.47
NORTH AMERICA (20 COUNTRIES)		7.7 SAINT LUCIA	20.71	CUBA	7.64
SOUTH AMERICA (12 COUNTRIES)		7.58 BRAZIL	12.8	PERU	3.31
AUSTRALIA (10 COUNTRIES)		5.23 N.COLEDONIA	12.8	SOLOMON ISL	0.58

Chart 13a

REGION WISE AVERAGE UNEMPLOYMENT % IN 2019

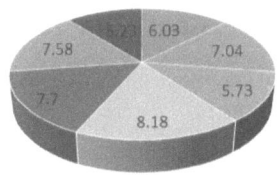

- UROPEAN UNION (26 COUNTRIES)
- EUROPE (42 COUNTRIES)
- ASIA (46 COUNTRIES)
- AFRICA (52 COUNTRIES)
- NORTH AMERICA (20 COUNTRIES)
- SOUTH AMERICA (12 COUNTRIES)
- AUSTRALIA (10 COUNTRIES)

Table 13 presents a picture of the total unemployment rate in the world as of 2019. COVID-19 has come on us as a bolt from the blue and has already created millions of new unemployment cases that are not highlighted in this book.

Table No. 14

REGION WISE MALE UNEMPLOYMENT %) IN THE YEAR 2019				
REGION	REGION WISE HIGHEST AND LOWEST % OF MALE UNEMPLOYMENT IN 2019.			
	HIGHEST	%	LOWEST	%
UROPEAN UNION (26 COUNTRIES)	GREECE	13.52	CONGO	1.57
EUROPE (42 COUNTRIES)	MACEDONIA	18.22	CZECH REP	1.57
ASIA (46 COUNTRIES)	PALESTINE	22.48	QATER	0.04
AFRICA (52 COUNTRIES)	SOUTH AFRICA	26.39	NIGER	0.56
NORTH AMERICA (20 COUNTRIES)	ST.VINCENT	20.39	CUBA	1.55
SOUTH AMERICA (12 COUNTRIES)	BROZEL	10.49	PERU	3.23
AUSTRALIA (10 COUNTRIES)	N.COLEDONIA	11.72	TONGO	0.53

Chart 14a

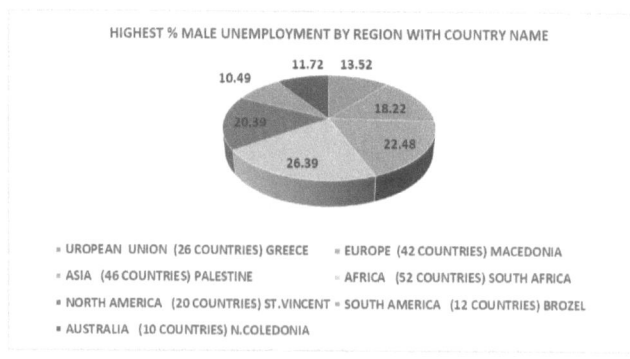

Chart 14b

LOWEST % MALE UNEMPLOYMENT BY REGION WITH COUNTRY NAME

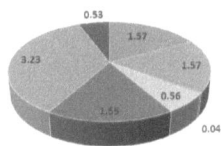

- UROPEAN UNION (26 COUNTRIES) GREECE 13.52 CONGO
- EUROPE (42 COUNTRIES) MACEDONIA 18.22 CZECH REP
- ASIA (46 COUNTRIES) PALESTINE 22.48 QATER
- AFRICA (52 COUNTRIES) SOUTH AFRICA 26.39 NIGER
- NORTH AMERICA (20 COUNTRIES) ST.VINCENT 20.39 CUBA
- SOUTH AMERICA (12 COUNTRIES) BROZEL 10.49 PERU
- AUSTRALIA (10 COUNTRIES) N.COLEDONIA 11.72 TONGO

Table No. 15

REGION WISE FEMALE UNEMPLOYMENT % IN THE YEAR 2019

REGION	REGION WISE HIGHEST AND LOWEST % OF FEMALE UNEMPLOYMENT IN 2019 - MALE			
	HIGHEST	%	LOWEST	%
UROPEAN UNION (26 COUNTRIES)	GREECE	22.02	CONGO	2.38
EUROPE (42 COUNTRIES)	GREECE	22.02	CRECH REP	2.38
ASIA (46 COUNTRIES)	PALESTINE	40.94	QATER	0.43
AFRICA (52 COUNTRIES)	SOUTH AFRICA	30.33	NIGER	0.36
NORTH AMERICA (20 COUNTRIES)	ST. LUCIA	23.26	CUBA	1.78
SOUTH AMERICA (12 COUNTRIES)	GUYANA	15.19	PERU	3.41
AUSTRALIA (10 COUNTRIES)	N.COLEDONIA	14.08	SOLOMON ISL	0.6

Chart 15a

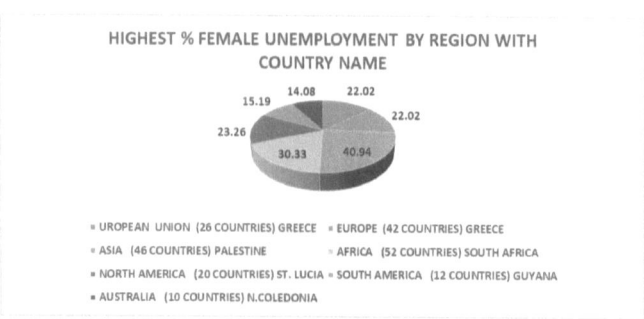

Chart 15b

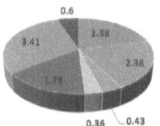

The world is in the clutches of the devastating coronavirus generated in Wuhan, China, in Asia. All nations in all regions have lost many lives, and it is still going on. Millions of working people of all category have lost their jobs. There is yet to be a total count.

From Table 13, we see that the total average unemployment rate in the world in 2019 is 7.04%, with the highest unemployment rate of 28.18% in South Africa. The highest male unemployment rate is 26.39% in South Africa (Table 14), and the highest female unemployment rate is 40.94% in Palestine (Table 15). Meanwhile, the lowest unemployment rate is 0.09% in

Qatar, in Asia. The lowest male unemployment rate is 0.04% in Qatar, and the lowest female unemployment rate is 0.36% in Niger, in Africa.

The highest unemployment rate of 8.18% is in Africa, followed by North America at 7.7%, South America at 7.58%, Europe at 7.04%, Asia at 5.73%, and Australia at 5.73%. It can be observed that female unemployment is much lower than the male population's. In Asia, the male to female unemployment ratio is around 1:2. The total unemployment rate in world regions is alarming; it has increased more due to the corona pandemic. It has posed a threat to the national and international economic structures.

To get away from the curse of unemployment, we have to adopt proper steps. We have to restructure the work culture and work atmosphere. To get national economic power, we have to divvy up jobs to every hand in our country. Towards the way of zero-balance unemployment, every boy and girl of working age must be appointed to a job.

But where are the jobs? We need to search for possible areas of employment opportunities. Yes, we have many things to do to save our society and to work for our nation. We need a dedicated group to save nature and our society from pollution.

Every year, we observe World Education Day on 24 January, yet we can't call ourselves a fully literate country. We need a dedicated group to spread literacy to every citizen in every corner of society.

Yes, to date, we observe World Health Day on 7 April, though certain groups of our citizens do not have proper health knowledge and information or proper treatment.

To date, we observe World Food Day every year on 16 October, yet a certain number of citizens do not even have food daily.

Tables 13 and 14 highlight the volume of the world's total unused workforce, the total unemployed population throughout the world countries. The huge national workforce is the actual strength of a nation in developing and strengthening the national and world economy. The development of a nation depends on demand, production, and consumption, and the world workforce is the force of total growth in the home economic system.

I mention in the 'Save, Spread, and Save' chapter that the spreading of salary to more and more hands is more judicious than a solid rise in pay to a certain group of people. It is not against the normal salary hike in way of increments and wage revisions. But surely the century demands employment in every hand to strengthen the economic system. Both wage revision and wage spreading are equally important. It is no loss to anyone, because, when a member of a family, who has attained the working age, will get his or her job in time. This is ultimately increasing the family income more than the ratio of wage hike. But as for the impact, along with the family finances, mental health gets stimulated, and the overall social national impact is really significant.

We have many elderly persons who have no one to look after them; we can reach out our hands and take care of them where required.

We can easily hand over the duty of maintaining a pollution-free, healthy society to the local youths, who will assist us in breathing comfortably, whilst at the same time, economic development will start to move upwards.

We get all benefits from society. We receive all our livelihood from the nature, but what do we give our society in return? What do we give nature in return? Say we don't look at its wellness at all. Today the time has come to spend for the society and nature. It's time to return back our love, our justice and safety to our society and nature. Thus, we and our future generations can survive and get benefit from pollution free nature.

When the reports of the social growth parameters come in black and white before us, we get hurt. We spent thousands of dollars on meetings, but the same result clouds us.

After a long period of education, training, workshops, etc., we get a merit certificate with a question mark in job possibilities. Later, we have a deep sigh in depression. Why that? Can we not engage the new energetic youths in nation building activities and gift them a better and happy life?

I hope we can. We can make them happy with a gift of an active life, providing them with an initial job cum training period of at least two years until they obtain a job of their preference. We can afford them a chance to serve for the homeland and the nation. On reaching sixteen or eighteen years of age, all life card holders should be offered a job in a *social service group*, with a salary in accordance with the common minimum daily wage structure.

Following the same strategy for all, students who have passed tenth or twelfth grade and who are at least sixteen or eighteen years of age should be handed over an appointment letter, along with his or her marks sheet and pass certificate, with an instruction to join the social service group in the locality where they live or near. It's like a part-time job with monthly salary, that will ease out the financial barriers of life and peace, keeping the chance to continue their study for better career building.

Equally a part of raising national feelings and love for society and nature, it needs to be a training period as well as a time for gathering experience and know the society and its needs and betterments. All boys and girls who have reached the age of sixteen or eighteen should be involved in national social work for a minimum of two years to know the society and to develop the integrity of the motherland, which will give them also financial protection and life support.

The same health card will be the control device that will ensure that all the boys and girls of the country are in an occupation. The same boys and girls, when they get a better job, will be appointed accordingly. They will be trained through short teacher training programmes, nursing training programmes, various health services, and other trainings free of cost so that they can render better service to society.

The society service group workers will be responsible for acting on the social needs of their locality, like:

a) teaching illiterate adults in the vicinity
b) assisting distressed old persons in need
c) commanding and monitoring the wastage of drinking water and electricity
d) overseeing surveillance of the local drainage system
e) teaching students from pre-primary to primary levels in distant regions
f) planting trees and gardening in the barren and unused lands as part of local beautification
g) offering health consultations and assistance to the common masses
h) assisting in schools and health centres.

COVID-19 has come as a scourge to migrant labour. I feel better employing the term *migrant* instead of *national*, and *labour* will be termed as *worker*—national workers. We in India are blessed with a really big national workforce. We need to employ our workforce in our production units and national infrastructure and civil works and production world.

We need to build up an area-specific centralised, disciplined, and registered workforce that has centralised identity cards in line with the national healthcare and national citizenship card. The national workforce will be provided a minimum of twenty-six days a month, with a daily salary as per government rate. All producers and public and private organisations of the country will hire manpower from the regional workforce centre.

Hence, when all citizens of the country are enrolled in a single controlled, centralised, and digitalised system, then there is no way to left out any worker from the job at any corner of a country. Then the dream of zero-balance employment is possible.

The system will strengthen the economy, yield the maximum production, and complete consumption. As the education will be provided to every corner of the country, along with healthcare starting from the birth of a child and to every student in school, there is no possibility of malnutrition or the unhealthy growth of a baby, and society will be gifted with a healthy workforce. Society will also get healthy mothers and healthy babies in the country.

The scheme will automatically reduce and minimise the national outlay on health. It will provide sound and bright scholars. Being part of social activities at the beginning of service life, every young boy and girl will be raised as dedicated workers of the motherland. It will reduce salary discrimination. As every working individual in the family will have a job, happiness and peace will spread in society. Morbidity rates in a society from every point, like domestic violence, malnutrition, child-death, disease, pollution, etc., will reduce. Pollution control and wastage reduction will save national income and strengthen the national economy.

CHAPTER SEVEN

SAVE, SPREAD, AND SAVE

A NATURE-FRIENDLY MOVEMENT TO STOP WASTAGE AND ABUSE

Cutting food waste is a delicious way of saving money, helping to feed the world and protect the planet.
Tristram Stuart

We have to follow and adopt a plan to save money and spread money to save the nation. Without money, nothing is possible. No wise economy will allow the printing of currency at random to overcome a fiscal crisis. But countries are facing the growth of populations by leaps and bounds.

Before going into detail, we have to find out some points, such as where and why we are fighting.

What is our need for connectedness? It's not an egg, to justify who came first, the hen or the orchis. Our primary objective is the evolution of the nation, as well as the globe. But it starts with the family. That is the basic unit of the society, which is in greater view builds the whole universe. What do we need to maintain a happy household? Foremost, we need to know our priority of actual and minimum sustaining needs. No exceptional thoughts and behaviours are taken into consideration.

Table No. 16

Common Human nature and target of livelihood and view of family within balanced Income			
	Nuclear family		Joint family
Family priority	father	Mother	Senior of family
Family income	Balanced	Balanced	Sufficient Jointly
Influence and Motivating factors	a) Importance	a) Passion	a) Gentility
	b) Responsibility	b) Responsibility	b) Passion
	c) Passion	c) Importance	c) Importance
Priority no 1st	Income	Food	Housing
Priority no 2nd	Food	Health	Education
Priority no 3rd	Health	Education	Health
Priority no 4th	Education	Income	food
Priority no 5th	Housing	Housing	Income
Priority no 6th	Savings	Savings	Savings

Human behaviour and priority in social life is influenced by the responsibility and motivation of the head of the family, within a balanced income in a nuclear family structure and a joint family structure.

Chart 16a

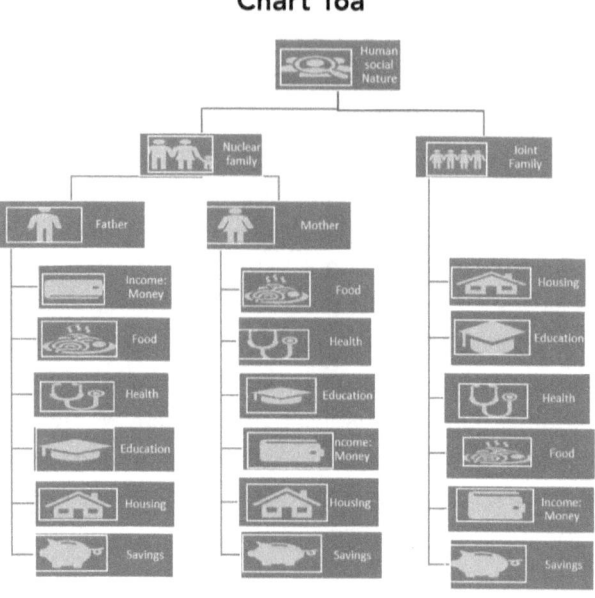

Practically all six targets dependent on each other are very essential to building up a smart nation. Priority varies depending on the point of view and financial condition of the executor of responsibility. No, in this chart, I have not considered another most important factor of human life, that is cloth. It is actually at the present generation that it is an integral part of health. Therefore, it is not highlighted separately.

There is a strange human nature and behaviour, that varies and works within the family members, depending on the nature of social responsibility, personal motivation, and family-target. A family runs in the force of the spirit of love, affection, and responsibility. Better, I start with the role of a father, in respect of the head of the family, yet it applies to a mother also when she is in the position of head of the household. He or she waits for their salary to be credited to their account. When it is received, they must go to the grocery store and vegetable market with a bag for food. Then they must buy things with a prescription for family medicines. And then he or she will pay the school and tuition fees of the children. The remainder will go to another part of their house maintenance, and then savings. It is because the head of the family is influenced by their duty and responsibility, which is then coated with passion and love for family members.

Whilst the duty and responsibility of family maintenance in the second stage is conferred to the mother, the point of view is shifted. In the hands of the mother, it will start with love and affection, and then duty and responsibility come into play. So it starts with food for the family, followed by health and education. Lastly, she will think of expenditure for housing and savings.

The whole point of view changes when the financial source is more than enough. The father and mother, along with other elders, are together to distribute funds for more secure living, with dignity and nobleness. The target changes, and they put housing first, then education. The priorities change because of the increase in the standard of living. That will help the family to belong in a better cultural environment. Then the cycle starts from health and food, and last comes income. Family behaviour is deeply motivated by the utility of livelihood, with the parameter of family income.

It is seen that health always comes as a second or third priority in any economic circumstance, but it never comes first. This is because if we have an active heart, only health and medicinal drugs are required.

Again, housing that is an essential means of subsistence for a surviving unit of a family has different substitutes, like a hotel, a rented house, office quarters, or office-provided accommodations. We can avail of rented houses as per our financial capability. Moreover, it takes a great amount of money that could be collected over a period of work and savings. In most instances, a family gets it ready as a family inheritance. For whom to save? Thus, in case of limited spending money, housing is less prioritized. But well-to-do family group enjoys housing as a priority, because it is then a status symbol of the family. However, the point is that the growth and elevation of a family depends on the supply of money. Income is the only source of money in any way, either through service or by other means. A family and its status and standard grow on economic growth. This economic growth rises with increases in the unit of earning members in the family by employment. At the same time, the savings of a family grows with the increase of earning heads.

At last, we see that savings is always the last priority for all common families, but practically, savings takes a major controlling as well as leading role in all the previous five steps, from beginning to end, in building up a successful, happy family. The savings ultimately gifts the family with successes and helps them reach the expected destination.

But why are these extraneous words of the very familiar family culture here?

A country is a collective figure of states. The state is a collective figure of families. Thus, no doubt the nation is a collective figure of all families within the provinces of the nation. Family economy depends on money, and the journey starts from income and ends at savings.

Overall administration of a country also depends on the priority list on different essential like support principle for its citizen. Similar to the growth of a family's standard and to economic growth, countries also need growth in the evolution of economic health, which is possible by raising the living standards of countrymen. We have to apply the essence of a smart and successful family to build up a smart and ideal country in true value.

Now we have to balance the coexistence of basic parameters that are the main constraints to achieving the goal. That means, either at the state level or country level, the national leader should act the part of head of the household. The leader should affectionately rule over the body politic and for the betterment of citizen, and his followers should execute service with love, discernment, and responsibility so that their service can motivate the countrymen to work for the development of the country with dedication.

We are earning; we are producing. Still, we can't take the complete benefits of that, because we can never fill the cup. It is too good to miss out on. It is wastage and loss.

Wastage and Loss

There is a report on global wastage published by FAO in 2014, called *Food Wastage Footprint: Full-Cost Accounting*. The final report reveals that about one-third of the worldwide production of consumables is being wasted. The cost of the wastage production, according to the report, is 1 trillion US dollars. This is just a portion of the direct total wastage disguised as economic cost. The shock and effect of this wastage on social cost and environmental damage is also considered very high. It multiplies the effect on every step of society and environment. It affects our nature, atmosphere, pollution, deforestation, natural resource, soil erosion, health, etc. It also creates wastage of man-hour, labour, and so on. As per report, it costs another 1.6 trillion USD for these wastages. The global annual wastage costs around minimum 2.6 trillion USD.

We are blind to it; we repeat this wastage year after year and ruin our national human and natural resources. In every field of life, we are wasting from morning to night, twenty-four hours a day, seven days a week. The future effect of this will be very alarming.

We need to save our universe from this alarming misuse of resources. We need to stop it here. We need not struggle over state and resources. We need to preserve our earth and resources. The enemy of our assets and gifts of nature is none other than us, all the countrymen who don't understand that our Tantalus cup will never run over until the hidden hole is shut.

We support various open and a few disguised reasons for such a high amount of loss and wastage. We dedicatedly should look after it and solve the obstructing issues to stop wastage.

I may at once attempt to bring forward the open and disguised obstacles to zero waste production and strengthen the national GDP, which we need to improve to build up a smart economy.

1) Anticipatory measure: During cultivation and production either it is a harvest of vegetable, one part of grain, or ingredients that spoil on the field or shop. It happens due to insects, moisture, natural calamities, manure, or neglect.

We strongly require advanced care, safe scientific and technical measures, and effective steps to save cultivation and production to ascertain a more beneficial and quality production by providing very healthy conditions, a healthy atmosphere, and the necessary amenities.

2) Post-production measures: Post-production and cultivation, collection, conveyance, and storage are major stages where the produced grains, vegetables, and products face damage, spoils, and insects.

Proper collection, transportation, storage, and arrangements to maintain and improve the quality of products are highly required for fresh products, grains, vegetables, and so on. Only this arrangement can stop wastage during the post-production and pre-processing period.

3) Processing period: A product, whether it is a vegetable or crop or manufactured consumable product, needs to process for consumption. Rice, pulses, and all food grains need to be refined in the husking mill. Then packing is done to send them out for consumption. Veggies, fish, milk, oils, etc.— the products are processed and placed in cold storage. During this preparation process, a portion of the product is destroyed and spoiled, and increases wastage of the commodities. Only a quick expert group of

workers and a suitable frost- and moisture-free storage system or cold storage with a reasonable temperature can save the products from decomposition. Wastage of fast-spoiling vegetables with fruits and fishery products raises the wastage rate high.
4) Expiry period: Most of the products have an expiry period. The materials or products need to be sold before the date of expiration. When it is not sold or consumed, it is thrown in the dustbin. Is it not wastage? A product, if not consumed, creates a big impact on the internal economic system.

To avoid wastage of consumables, the product, once ready for consumption, should reach the hands of the consumer in time. So a proper retailing system of the product in the proper locality with its actual customer group should be built. A village without electricity cannot purchase a refrigerator or washing machine. A kids' garment shopkeeper can't sell kids' products if there is no child in the neighbourhood.

Any commodity or product is an outcome of a group of things—some visible and some invisible, some material and some non-material, some accountable and some unaccountable. All these are the essential ingredients of the product. Consider a cake; the essential and visible elements or ingredients in it are flour, sugar, eggs, baking powder, butter or oil, salt, fruits, a packaging box, etc. a combined expenditure of fund and natural resources. When these are lost or decomposed, it destroys more than we expect.

The toil, the expertise, and the designing are invisible, but they are accountable elements by unit, hour, and cost. However, we cannot count the economic involvement of the quantity of influence of nature that has been used for the production of the eggs, fruits, flour, and so on. The cost of all visible and invisible elements and ingredients are involved in production of a material. Even the post-wastage decomposition, pollution of the unused products, and accountable misuse of labour and man-hours cost more. Altogether, these agents, when tallied one to one with a unit of money for any single unit of product wasted by any means, give us pain. Money, natural influence, manpower lost, fuel, and labour cost are invested in the products. Various types of natural resources and environmental elements, directly and indirectly involved, are out of our anticipation. When accumulated and counted in terms of money, these all will show the real wastage. This will actually exceed the total wastage, more than one-third estimated.

At last, I would like to focus the spotlight on a few disguised losses and regular wastage, with the intention of further purification and rectification in our total human work culture, to construct a quiet and good atmosphere, and an environment of production.

A) **Poor management and maintenance:** The poor and inadequate management and maintenance plays a major part in wastage. On that point are sometimes social, natural, and economic reasons that create a loss of workforce and man-hours in way of labour unrest, bandh, lock-out, closures, strikes, and so on.

The workers and labourers are not solely responsible for these occurrences of agitation in the production house. These are sometimes the reactions and outcomes of conflict because of the unawareness, impassivity, and obstinacy on the part of management towards workers' health, security, financial and social commitment, and fights for the struggle of the existence of the workers. The wrong decisions, vindictive attitude and actions, greediness, partiality, and prejudiced management decisions go against the manpower. These instances of agitation create lesser and delayed production, and they destroy the stock of commodities for production. In many cases, these also lead to the destruction and decomposition of stored raw materials, especially of vegetables and short-life products. A short supply of low-quality food grains leads to low-quality production. Such problems create losses and wastage of consumable merchandise. These cause low production and cause a price hike of the finished products, which causes less consumption. Wastage increases. Good relations, an administration with positive approach, compassionate behaviour with dignity, and maintaining proper welfare activities for the workers can prevent this problem. There are many organisations in India and world countries where there is a very happy atmosphere and good relations between the men and management.

B) **Production by unskilled workers:** In many cases, whether by the pressure and demand of local people to maintain less production cost or by political pressure, companies become bound to appointing unskilled workers. The manufacturing defects increase; at the same time, quantity of production decreases, and wastage increases.

It is a very common factor, and we cannot avoid it until employment for all is generated. This is the outcome of the struggle of existence that has started from the beginning of human society. Proper training for unskilled workers can solve the problem of low-quality and lesser-quantity production. The cost of training as a whole is very minimal compared to the monetary value of continuous loss and wastage of products.

C) **Flagitious wastage:** It is an abnormal and very peculiar, sensitive, cold-blooded wastage of national production, with a wide scope of influence within a country. The intentional market manipulation has much influence and effect on the total national GDP. There are some businessmen and leaders in the country who only run after high profit by way of unpolished methods. They generally crack the common supply chain of essential commodities.

To get a higher price for commodities and to earn higher profit, they store and hide the products, usually common daily essentials and regular consumable goods. In this manner, a fictitious crisis in product supply is generated, and the unit cost of a product increases in the marketplace. This type of hoarding and storing ultimately creates a massive wastage and degradation in product quality; it is a common method known as black marketing. It pushes the product price up, but the product loses its purity and becomes a threat to health. Therefore, it not only pushes up wastage; it also brings health hazards to the consumers.

D) **Choice:** The next thing that influences wastage is choice. Everywhere, choice becomes a great source of huge wastage. Choice in brand, product, and quality leads to wastage of common merchandise. Food, vegetables, dresses, clothes, beddings, and even cosmetics—every consumable product has its consumer. It depends on the likes and dislikes of a man or woman, and on their consumption power, status, and need.

Only a better production atmosphere and quality production system and study of consumer behaviour can reduce the wastage of consumable products. All this wastage harms every level of the production system.

1) There is an increase in the product price of every unit. To keep pace with the demand of customers for a product, an extra set of production facilities and extra investments are required.
2) To keep pace with the scheduled investment, customer demand will be discounted. Production will decrease and will be insufficient for customers. To keep step with marketplace demand and brand prestige, the cost has to be hiked, and they will have to lose customers.
3) Extra manpower and man-hours are required to satisfy the need and supply gap. Extra natural resources are needed to create additional production. Due to excessive work pressure, the farmers and labourers will suffer from wellness problems.
4) The wastage leads to some extra production to cover up the market demand. It causes pressure of extra investment of fund, social, and environmental effect. It also causes effect on natural resources like land, water, soil, etc. and the natural minerals and fuels. The effect of such wastage leads to change in nature. Deforestation, droughts, global warming, scarcity of

water and fuel, and so on are marching the world towards destruction.

Impact of Wastage in Production Cost and Product Price

We have to keep in mind that every unit of wastage in consumable products ensures the obvious and compulsory loss of some percentage of our manpower, money, and materials. *Materials* refers to natural resources, like water, air, electricity, soil, coal, minerals, chemicals, natural and ground oils, etc. At the same time, inevitable compensatory investment of another sets the same percentage of all manpower, money, and materials to cover up the loss of that unit and to equilibrate the demand and supply of the consumer. Thus, every one unit of loss puts pressure on the natural resources and the workforce. It actually enhances the overuse of natural resources. It adversely affects the production world. It also highly affects the product price determination as a whole. The result is an increase in the market price of that product.

Figure G1

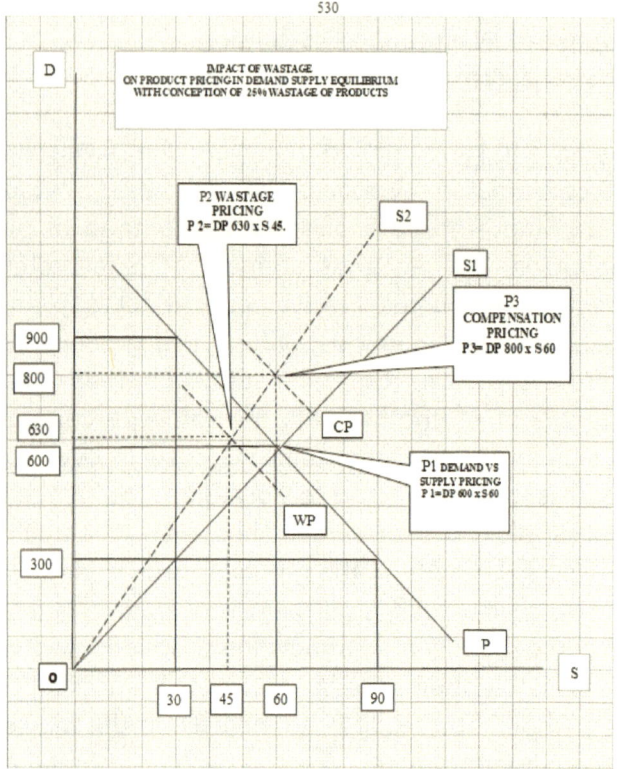

In Figure G1, I have attempted to highlight how subtly the demand-versus-supply equilibrium pricing factor is affected and influenced in increasing the product unit cost.

In this graph of demand and supply pricing equilibrium, we may consider the common behaviour and principle of market in respect of investment, production, demand, and supply.

POST-CORONA ECONOMY

Suppose a producer has invested some fund with a target of some consumable product. As per law of demand and supply he has to produced 60 unit of the product. At P1 S1 production and supply equilibrium point, he has produced 60 unit at Rs 600.00 per unit.

Now, we consider the average 25% wastage of production (in place of wastage @ $1/3^{rd}$ of production as per published report). The outcome of short supply of 15 unit will create an uncertainty in supply vs demand in market. It will compel the producer to re-think on pricing of balance production or to produce the product to manage market demand, to avoid financial loss. But the wastage effect pushes the product pricing point. A new equilibrium price point is generated at P2 in the S2 supply curve, with a total quantity of 45 units after a 25% wastage effect, total of 15 units. The new equilibrium price to compensate financial loss becomes 630 rupees per unit.

At present, with the total projected unit of demand versus supply being 90 units, the balance wastage unit of 22.5 units will require another set of compensatory expenditure in MMM, i.e. manpower, money, and materials. The ultimate result is that the total wastage cost, including all groups of expenses, and another set of additional compensatory production costs will force the total expenditure. It will automatically invite a rise in the unit cost of total output. P3 is the new compensatory equilibrium pricing point of 800 rupees per unit of a total of 90 units. So a product with the actual price of 600 rupees, we will get it at

800 rupees—around 33.3% extra wastage burden. In this way, wastage silently spreads to human life and the production world. The product market price will increase with every point of increasing wastage.

We have to reduce wastage. We have to save some part of 2.6 trillion US dollars by reducing the loss of one-third of production. We can reduce the product price and over-extraction and overconsumption of national resources.

Hence, our role and responsibility should be removing the wastage and saving the economy. Stop abusing. Save wealth. Save nature, save life. Save life, save the universe.

Spread

In the previous part, I tried to emphasise the saving of funds at a micro level. The basic view of the society is to bring happiness in our family life. We therefore try to buy our happiness and peace in family by small individual savings in money and in kinds to protect our future life. In domestic field we try to save by avoiding loss and wastage of money and goods.

We have to generate funds. We need to deliver a solid economy. It is possible only when we can dole out cash in hand.

The common economic system says when *demand* increases, *supply* increases. This demand is expressed in the terms *consumption*, *purchase*, and *sale*. All three terms are regulated by the consumer, purchaser, and customer, and are maintained by their income. On the other hand, supply is expressed in *production*. So to increase funds, we must generate income and consumers. Only increasing consumers will increase consumption, which will inspire production and supply. We therefore need to spread income. Increasing salaries or income does not always increase consumption; rather, it helps increase *savings*. Savings is another pillar of a sound economic system. But the power of an economy is in consumption. The use of trade goods directly encourages an increase in supply and production. Having savings is human nature. For how many consumers will be generated, an equal quantity of savings will be brought forward; at the same time, consumption and the consumer will be generating more.

Let us see the human habit of domestic savings throughout the world.

In Table 17 below, we see the domestic savings habits of the World Bank income groups of employees from the year 2000 to 2018. We see that the total savings percentage of the GDP of the high-income group and upper-middle-income group in the year 2018 is 23.227% and 32.369%, respectively. Again, the cumulative figure of GDP percentage of savings as per statistics is as follow. The middle-income group contributed 30.728%, lover-middle-income group contributed 23.424% in the year 2019, low- and middle-income group contributed 30.537%, and low-income group of employees contributed

15.210% in the year 217 respectively, the cumulative figure of GDP percentage is savings. Thus, we can easily say that the low- to middle-income groups of the population are higher contributors than the high- and upper-middle-income groups.

Table No. 17

POPULATION : DOMESTIC SAVINGS HABIT% OF GDP & POPULATION GROWTH IN WORLD BANK INCOME GROUP							
GROSS DOMESTICS SAVINGS HABIT GDP %					POPULATION GROWTH		
World Bank Income Group	2000	2010	2018		2000	2010	2018
World Savings Rate	25.477	25.093	25.281		6.114	6.922	7.674
High income Group	24.028	21.425	23.227		1.101	1.179	1.236
Upper middle Income group	30.181	36.073	32.369		5.013	5.743	6.438
Middle Income Group	29.203	34.312	30.728		0.4214	0.5313	0.6685
Lower Middle income Group	25.142	27.153	*23.424	*2019	2.156	2.548	2.913
Low income Group	13.575		*15.21	*2017	2.455	2.663	2.856

Table No. 18

REGION WISE TOTAL SAVINGS IN BILLION USD WITH HIGHEST AND LOWEST IN THE YEAR 2018					
	SAVINGS	HIGHEST		LOWEST	
TOTAL COUNTRIES IN REGION	USD	COUNT	USD	COUNTRY	USD
WORLD		160.57	CHINA 6294.1	LIBERIA	-2.09
EUROPEAN UNION	27	148.46	GERMA 1156.9	MALTA	4.49
EUROPE	41	135.96	GERMA 1156.9	MONTENEGRO	0.82
ASIA	35	315.7	CHINA 6294..11	BHUTAN	0.53
AFRICA	37	8.50	NIGEER 76.59	LIBERIA	2.29
NORTH AMERICA	13	346.39	USA 3817.1	BELIZE	0.16
SOUTH AMERICA	10	51.78	BRAZIL 233.46	GUYANA	1.37
AUSTRALIA	3	119.76	AUSTRA 311.71	BRUNEI	7.35

As per TheGlobalEconomy.com (Table 18), global savings in the year 2018 were 160.57 billion USD. China, in Asia, had the highest in annual savings rate, with a total of 6,294.11 billion USD, and Liberia, in Africa, had the lowest in this race, saving 2.09 billion USD. For annual savings rates in 2018, North America, with thirteen countries, was the highest, with a total savings of 346.39 billion USD, with the USA as the highest saver of a total of 3,817.08 billion USD. Asia, with thirty-five nations (including India, China, Bangladesh, Nepal, Bhutan, etc.), was the second highest, with an average savings rate of 315.96 billion USD. Then, by order of savings rate, came Europe, Australia, South America, and lastly, Africa, with a savings rate of only 8.50 billion USD.

From Table 19, we can find the difference amongst all income groups in sharing contributions in national economic growth. We find the following data on Annual growth of population and GDP growth of income groups, published by the World Bank National Accounts Data and OECD National Accounts Data.

The data reveals that the world's annual growth percentage in GDP of the World Bank income groups was 3.098% in 2018 and 2.475% in 2019, which has downsized from 4.385 in year 2000, having many ups and downs during past eighteen years.

Table No. 19

WORLD BANK ANNUAL GDP: GROWTH % & TOTAL POPULATION GROWTH %											
INCOME GROUP GDP %							POPULATION GROWTH %				
World Bank Income Group	2000	2005	2010	2015	2018	2019	2000	2005	2010	2015	2018
World Savings Rate	4.385	3.195	4.301	2.879	3.098	2.475	1.323	1.247	1.204	1.169	1.105
High income Group	4	2.9	2.9	2.3	2.3	1.7	0.6	0.7	0.7	0.6	0.5
Upper middle Income group	6	7.100	7.6	3.6	4.5	3.8	0.9	0.8	0.7	0.8	0.7
Middle Income Group	5.6	7	7.5	4	4.7	3.9	1.4	1.2	1.2	1.1	1.1
Lower Middle income Group	4.2	6.6	6.9	5.7	5.2	4.4	1.8	1.7	1.6	1.5	1.4
Low income Group	2.9	6.9	5.8	2.1	3.6	3.9	2.7	2.8	2.6	2.5	2.6

The global rate of annual population growth in the World Bank income groups has reduced to 1.105% in 2018, from 1.323% in 2000.

The table highlights that the annual percentages of GDP growth in the high-income group in 2018, 2.03%, and 2019, 1.7%, have downsized compared to the year 2000, with a rate of 4%. The upper-middle-income group was at 4.5% in 2018 and 3.8% in 2019, having downsized from 6% in 2000. The global rate of annual population growth, at the same time, has reduced to 0.5% and 0.7% in 2018, from 0.6% and 0.9% in 2000.

The data on contribution in annual growth percentage in GDP during 2018 and 2019 by different income group is shown here.

The data highlights that, the middle-income group in 2018 and 2019 have contributed 4.7% and 3.9%, low-income group – 3.6% and 3.9%, and lower middle-income group 5.2% and 4.4%, while the contribution rate in the year 20000 was 5.6%, 2.9%, and 4.2% respectively.

The annual percentage of GDP growth of population are, middle-income group in 2015 and 2018 is 1.1% and 1.1%, low-income group – 2.5% and 2.6%, and lower middle-income group 1.5% and 1.4%. The same in the year 2000 was respectively 1.4%, 2.7%, and 1.8%

The above statistics justify that the low- to middle-income groups of populations are the chief contributors in national growth in the world in annual GDP percentage growth, and are also the largest population groups under the World Bank income groups. Being the smallest population group, participation in national economic growth in the national production world, annual savings, annual use, etc. are really limited for the high-income group and upper middle-income group of a population.

It proves that if we want to reach real self-reliance, we have to look towards the low- to middle-income groups of a population for its growth and spread. The growth is not quantified in terms of money or salary growth. Growth is quantified in the number of the population, which means appointments. Each and every unit of growth at this degree will benefit from total economic growth by an increment in production, expenditure, and savings.

After examining the tables on common human behaviour, domestic savings habits, total savings rates by the World Bank income groups, annual percentage growth in GDP, and annual population growth rate, we have to make the practical and progressive decision.

It is the prime thing; we have to find out solution to solve it and to establish the entire economic growth of the nation. On the other hand, increasing salaries leads to more savings, but the savings habit of humankind is of two kinds: (1) idle savings and (2) active savings or banks. So spreading income is more welcome than increasing income, to establish a healthy economy and healthy companionship. The comparative study below will help demonstrate the power of consumption and savings.

Savings	Consumption
Savings is one of the passive supports of a healthy economy to strengthen a country's economic system.	Expenditure is the active and direct resource of a healthy economy to strengthen a country's economic system and power.
Savings create an idle fund for the time being, it is like holding and carrying cash in hand. It helps generate a banking fund.	Consumption is an active fund that influences and builds up economic power manifold. It strengthens the connection to your ideal market.
Savings has a passive part in the country's economy and acts slowly for national development through the banking system.	Consumption has an active role in the economy. It directly takes part in national development, being the liquid cash flow in the hands of businessmen and shop owners.

It is a slow process of national development. Consumers are the key figures of the fund but possess no direct function or capacity in spending for production.	It is the speedy process of national development. Consumers have direct involvement in increasing production and national growth.
A percentage of collective savings in banks comes into the market through the path of investment and then comes into the production role.	Every unit of daily consumption turns to liquid money to run a grocery store. It directly gets into the national production role in building up purchasing capacity.
Savings indirectly prevents money flow into the market and curbs purchasing power for the time being.	Consumption directly supplies business money. It helps with growth in the economy of the nation.
Savings is the genuine source of the banking system. It aids in large investments in the production world and creates a specialist workforce for quality and sound yield.	Consumption indirectly creates money for savings by influencing growth in business and generating consumers by increasing employment. It helps in increasing bank savings.
It influences rich persons to invest and helps businessmen operate a commercial enterprise on a large scale to strengthen the internal economic system.	It acts on poor and rich persons to be components of national growth and income, and at the same time, it influences income and savings in the long run.

Savings is, in real terms, a source of big investments and less employment. Any big investment always needs maximum time to come into the production field and run by technology, and it creates less employment in the country.	Consumption of commodities and services is, in real terms, the actual source of market finance. It creates investment power of small scale business and daily market places. This investment is the genuine force of the economic system, because it helps spread the money, increasing manpower.
Savings ensures the security of future days for a family. It also helps the country by building up viable funds for business growth and other important financial acitivities.	Consumption helps spread and increase savings. With the number of increases in employment, the same number of saving units increases, so consumption is a direct source of bank funds also.
High-income group savings	**Low-income group savings**
Maintaining a livelihood is very common in high- and low-income groups. The basic needs of humans are all but the same. The difference comes in terms of the brands of products consumed; costly living facilities are used by the high-income group.	The low-income group also demand the same food, medical apparel, etc. The only difference is in the choice of brands and comparatively low-priced products. It does not change much.

POST-CORONA ECONOMY

Savings is a general and common habit of human beings. But it depends on the expenditure needs of a family and the family status. So far, other than exceptional events, most people try to save a certain percentage of their income. Actually, the high-income group of a country saves less than the low-income group as a whole. The total count depends on the number of heads in the high-income group.	The low-income group are bigger than the high-income group. Being higher in number, the cumulative total savings is also high. For instance, if one high-income person saves 20 rupees per day and consumes fifty units of products per day, a total of ten high-income people save 200 rupees per day and consume a total of five hundred units of products. At a ratio of 1:20, the low-income group saves just 10 rupees per day and consumes only forty units of products per day. Two hundred low-income people save 2,000 rupees a day and consume a total of eight thousand units of products per day.
The high-income group and the upper-middle-income group of the population, being lesser in quantity than the low-to middle-income group, have less influence and enactment in national production in quantity, but they are the final and prime controller of production quality. That helps in the research and evolution of any merchandise.	The cumulative number of total low-income group, lower middle-income group, and low-income group of population are total 12.2% of GDP. It is higher than total cumulative number of populations in high-income group and upper-middle-income group with a total 5.5% of GDP.

	Therefore, the low-income group, lower middle-income group, and low-income group have the controlling power over output development and expansion in the production world. They are the highest consumer of the national products and services. They influence the growth in demand and supply through highest consumption and savings. It influences the common market and total employment.
A certain percentage of the savings of the high-income group goes to savings on the purchase of non-productive goods, like gold, jewellery, and all other costly ornaments. Therefore, it becomes a non-productive investment and has the least impact on economic growth.	The low-income group of employees mostly uses money for daily consumable products and the most important commodities to to maintain smooth family life with daily bread and butter. Then they think of housing and savings. Costly gold and jewellery are fashion items to them. Thus, they become direct investors in the economic world through low savings.

The high-income group is the least in quantity, but a great part of the group is responsible for the majority of wastage and abuse of daily consumable products produced in a state. They provide the least share in building an economy and a nation.	The low-income group is alerted of wastage due to their scarcity of everyday needs and hand-to-mouth economic conditions. They are the most common buyers of common products in the grocery store. Being the actual savings group and highest in number, they provide a majority of the shares in the economy.

Both savings and consumption are essential for the development of a country. At the same time, we want a country where no one is without food, health, and a happy shelter. Therefore, we need a zero-balance workforce and a very powerful economic system that can make us boldly say that we are one, that we are united.

I have tried to say that we need to circulate money. We have to reach money to every hand, like health and education. Not a single youth of working age will be devoid of work. But it is not like alms or donations. It should be a prestigious remuneration for serving. We must spread money to every hand by way of providing work for everyone.

When everyone has their job and every job has its worker, then no economy will have to look back. When every hand sustains a line of work, then every corner of the state, whether urban or rural, will have the light of knowledge, light of strength, light of happiness, light of health, and light of graceful refinement.

Save Nature, Save the Country, Save the Universe

Now I come to the last phase of the chapter. It is again *save*. Save in a broader perspective.

Save society by way of saving nature and by saving the natural resources of the earth. The sources of raw materials and natural resources are limited to keep pace with the balance between demand and supply of a growing population. Natural resources are decreasing abundantly. World countries are no longer dependent on only agricultural output. Today the universe is running on substitutes and consumption variety. Nations are now not exclusively used for agriculture. Human residences and industries are increasing regularly. So we just have to search out further and alternative ways to keep pace with the situation.

Yes, it is possible through only the judicious utilisation of natural resources. We have to control our consumptive behaviour. We can't refuse, that the situation is created by human race. It also indicates an acute global affliction problem in the days of our antecedents. We the nations are all fighting over a Tantalus cup and may continue fighting. We have to think of our country; we have to feel for our country. We must hold a deep passion for our nation.

POST-CORONA ECONOMY

We have to work together to save our country. To build a better economy, we have to chant the mantra *'Save'*. Save at every point of our lifespan. We are now fighting over a Tantalus cup English to Bengali dictionary PDFeiii social, cultural, and economic life, and in the production world. Then we can stop the unwanted loss of all types of natural resources, from the bottom of the ocean to the sky.

We can preserve wildlife; we can save the plant world. We can also preserve our valuable forests. We can save our cultivation and production world. We can enjoy the pollution-free clear blue sky all day long. By stopping *wastage* and *loss*, we can save trillions in national funds. Reducing health hazards at an early period, we can start a health program and save trillions of lives and national funds by reducing national medical expenditure. By providing health-based education, we can generate a healthy and talented society, and a very smart workforce that will cause our national as well as world production to flourish in quality and quantity. We can offer a job at every hand from the saved money and welcome a smart, clean, light, and pollution-free society without welcoming any inflation. We can bring a renaissance to the production world and gift a *zero*-balance society with education, health, and employment, and save the universe from the curse of negativities. We can be proud of enjoying self-reliance in the actual condition and pass around our friendship to our world counterparts with open minds and smiling faces in sharing our culture, pedagogy, and expertise with each other.

Let international friendships reach the level where we can meet and enjoy other countries that are usually seen in common tourist books. But self-reliance is a winner.

CHAPTER EIGHT

SELF-RELIANCE

A VISION AND MISSION TOWARDS SELF-DEPENDENCE

You cannot help people permanently by doing for them what they could and should do for themselves.
Abraham Lincoln

Do we not realize that self-respect comes with self-reliance?
A. P. J. Abdul Kalam

Way towards Self-Reliance

World countries are, at present, very busy building up self-reliance. World superpowers, having their viable and commendable economic stability and strength, are now stepping forward to build up an irresistible and unparalleled supersonic power. Every country must have the right and necessity to build up the power to fight against an unexpected enemy of the state.

But for this aim, every country needs to attain self-reliance in all components of life. Unless we come out of dependence on another nation, we can't achieve all-out self-reliance.

To achieve self-reliance, the country needs to be firm in the basic human power development plan. That is possible when every one of the states is sufficiently strong in knowledge, health, and sustenance. Confidence in society will grow only when society has complete mental and physical support and satisfaction. A nation, consequently, needs to be made up of a very potent, healthy, educated, and established human power and united national strength.

'A hungry crow cannot crow.' We have to keep in mind that a hungry human being needs food first. It will afford them the grand capability to make up their mental confidence level. Only a man who has secured basic needs in life and mental support, like

health, work, education, and a house, can think for some advanced area of life.

The word *strong* is applied in a wider sense. Strong manpower means it is a manpower moderately sound in education and strong in physical and mental health. It is free from all diseases and illnesses, within a peaceful atmosphere and environment that may make the essence of good feelings on social ideologies and moralities in one's personal life.

For self-reliance, we need a very powerful economy. The economic growth of a country depends on the production of consumption. The production, in cyclic order, increases production, consumption, and income.

To achieve the dream of self-reliance, we need education for all, food for all, health and medical aid for all, a roof for all, and also a job for all. The main weapon in building a society depends on literacy, food, shelter, medicines, and consumable income for a secure, peaceful life.

When a society, as well as a nation, reaches the destination of zero balance in education, food, medical aid, shelter, and jobs, the guild will gain mental and moral strength, as well as be powered by self-reliance. No divisive evil power would be able to vote out a strong and confident nation.

The concept of a happy life and a happy family can gear up with overall satisfaction and self-dependence.

Health

A nation can't survive if the nation is not physically fit to fight all obstacles to survival. Thus, we first need to establish a healthy society by providing sufficient health support from cradle to grave.

The kids are the focal point of a healthy body politic. The newborn child is a future citizen. If every child grows up with proper physical and medical support, the nation cannot be unhealthy.

Active attention is highly required to find a policy for development in the health sector. We can have a look through a few morbidity records of children under five years of age, published by the World Bank, WHO, OECD, etc.

Table No. 20

Child-death below 5 yr from the low health facility

Child Mortality Causes	2000 No	2010 No	2017 No
Child Wasting	950,629	606,161	425,927
Indoor pollution for solid fuel	590,962	357,580	229857
Outdoor Pollution	233,806	179,454	141,691
Child stunning	322,548	188,947	119,037
Child Underweight	265,655	149,639	92,690
No access to handwash facility	182,081	124,705	90,494
Low birth weight	114,836	86,164	62,875
Second-hand smoking	170,547	90,483	61,348
Non-exclusive breastfeeding	135,120	84,287	60,276
Vitamin A Deficiency	133,690	79,039	52,862
Zink deficiency	36,195	20,047	12,377

Child-death below 5 yr from other health causes and diseases

Child Mortality Causes	2000 No	2010 No	2017 No
Lower Respiratory infection	1.68 M	1.12M	808920
Congenital Birth defect	664545	578826	501764
Malaria	567847	500074	354294
Other Neonatal disorder	498728	430205	349002
Neonatal Spine Infection	237914	224578	203013
Meningitis	266781	190512	153058
Nutritional deficiencies	367097	217837	145073
Whooping Cough	138048	100537	86091
Measles	478728	153567	83439
HIV/AIDS	245759	169361	77485
Tuberculosis	132222	81039	57370
Cancer	58953	51270	49916

The chart shows what happens to a child after birth. The death rate and morbidity rate could be reduced by preventing the causes of death by providing sure, suitable, and sufficient medical attention and documentation. The girl child especially will be taken care of in a progressive way so that, in the long run, they will become the healthy mother of a healthy child. To reduce premature death, we need to take all-out steps to eliminate the morbidity causes in a proper and justified manner.

Education

Today all the countries in the world are trying to spread education. Unfortunately, there is still a long way to go. We can see below that the World Bank published a report on children out of reach of basic primary education on different economic and social conditions. The data on both boys and girls out of school around the world is very alarming, and it is a great barrier to building up a smart, healthy society throughout the world. To build up self-reliance, the nation first needs an educated and healthy human force in society.

Table No. 21

CHILDREN OUT OF SCHOOL % AT PRIMARY SCHOOL AGE						
REGION	2000	2010	2018	2000	2010	2018
	BOYS IN %			GIRLS IN %		
World	12.366	8.495	7.184	17.741	9.839	9.263
High income countries	3	2	2	4	2	2
Upper middle-income countries	4	3	3	5	3	3
Middle income countries	10	8	6	15	8	8
Lower middle-income countries	15	11	8	24	12	11
Low income countries	39	18	16	49	24	21

What is the reason for this when even food is being supplied to bring the students to school? Is the weakness of the national economy behind poor literacy? The answer is no. Today every developed and developing country is trying its best to wipe out illiteracy from the country. Nevertheless, it is sure that money is the primary cause behind poor literacy. In the table, it is shown that 2% of boys and girls in high-income groups are out of school from nursery to primary education age. The number of out-of-school children is gradually increasing in the low-income group. Moreover, girl children are more likely than boys to be out of school.

For reference, I am giving a chart of annual expenditure at GDP percentage for national education at the government level of some countries.

Table No. 22

GOVT. EXPENDITURE PRIMARY & SECONDARY EDUCATION GDP % PER STUDENT				
	PRIMARY		SECONDARY	
REGION	GDP %	YEAR	GDP %	YEAR
WORLD	15.562	2013	20.08	2013
UK	24.2	2016	21.2	2016
USA	19.9	2016	21.1	2016
S AFRIKA	17.9	NA	21.4	2018
INDIA	9.8	2013	16.9	2013
PAKISTAN	8.1	2105	16	2015
CHINA	7.6	2013	11.4	1999
BANGLADESH	7.6	2009	9.9	2016

It is the scarcity of money in the hands of poor households. When even one piece of bread is not regularly available to some families, how can we expect a family to allow the children to go to school?

Both father and mother are out of the house to look for rations.

Do we expect the child to come to school alone when his or her parent is out? Practically, no parent will send their child alone to school. It is the original fact and a very normal lifestyle.

So in most cases, the boy and the girl child learn different ABCs and take an active part in the struggle of the existence of the family. These ABCs are nothing but *alms*, *bread*, and *cooking*, because it is the fate of life before the innocent children.

We, from the childhood try to, provide literacy. The family first needs some financial power in hand to spare for the child to attend class, not only to attend the day the food is supplied by the school. Poor families cannot reach for money, so money should reach the poor family to improve their social strength.

At the same time, a poor family has no way to get medical facilities for their children or even for themselves. Thus, the children inevitably suffer from malnutrition and poor health. A poor family cannot reach the health programme with the children, so medical aid must reach towards the poor family to bring them under a health programme.

We have to look through corner to corner of society to bring every single unit into the group of a healthy family, a healthy society. A family is a part of a society, as well as a part of a country. So a happy, healthy, and literate family as a whole creates a happy, healthy, and educated society and a smart country.

Financial Power

Job and Income

Then comes the question of financial power—in other words, a job and a source of money. It is only financial power that can help poor men to get literate defeating the natural and geographical barriers. Financial power will help to maintain a happy and healthy life by way of self-dependency. So, every man attaining the service age, should have to provide with a job in hand. It will generate demand, that will push for production and supply. It will help to strengthen national economy.

To distribute job in every hand is highly essential to revive the economic downfall of the nations caused by Corona Pandemic. We have to find out the scope of services and appointments. We have to expand job opportunities. We need to general consumer. An automatic cycle of economic growth through demand, production, supply, and consumption will influence the production growth and will insist for new appointments.

Only a smart, healthy, and educated society can gain self-reliance. A society that has financial power in every hand, earned by its own labour, can dream of good education and good health. If a society gets all three powers—i.e. knowledge earned through education, physical power earned through proper and timely medication, and financial power earned through knowledge and physical power and a job in hand—the nation cannot be stopped. The moral strength in the population, raised by education, health, and work in hand, will boost self-reliance.

CHAPTER NINE

WORKERS' REST HOUSE 'JATIYA KARMI AWAS'

A ROOF WITH HEALTH SUPPORT FOR NATIONAL WORKERS

POST-CORONA ECONOMY

The COVID-19 pandemic has now brought forth another suppressed social problem that has been highlighted by the corona outbreak. That is a roof for the worker, i.e. a safe living facility.

The sudden coronavirus attack and sudden closure of all business activities and productions have come as a curse to the group of workers, called migrant labour, who are the backbone of national progress.

There are millions of skilled and unskilled workers in the country. No, I am not using the term *labour* as having multiple meanings. They are also not migrants from other countries. They are, in the broader sense and in our terms, Indian, and they are an integral part of our Indian nationality. The term I am using for this group is *national workers*. This may be said in Bengali as *Jatiya Karmi*. No, they do not come from other countries or any other universe. They are our countrymen within our Indian territory. They could be from other states, but they are working for our national progress.

There may be various opinions about these national workers, their working capacities, and their abilities, but surely we need them. They are the main workforce.

I wish to mention the total workforce available in our world, scattered throughout the regions. Commonly, the working-age group of a population is defined on different age scales in different countries. However, it is generally considered to range from fifteen years old to sixty-five years old.

A chart of the labour force available within the working-age group is presented here for awareness of the severe effect of the COVID-19 pandemic on the labour world.

Table No. 23

WORKING AGE GROUP OF POPULATION		
	TOTAL POPULATION	YOUNG GROUP
High income Group	54	25
Low income Group	45	31
Lower Middle-income Group	51	39
Middle Income Group	57	47
Upper middle-Income group	83	76

Chart 23a

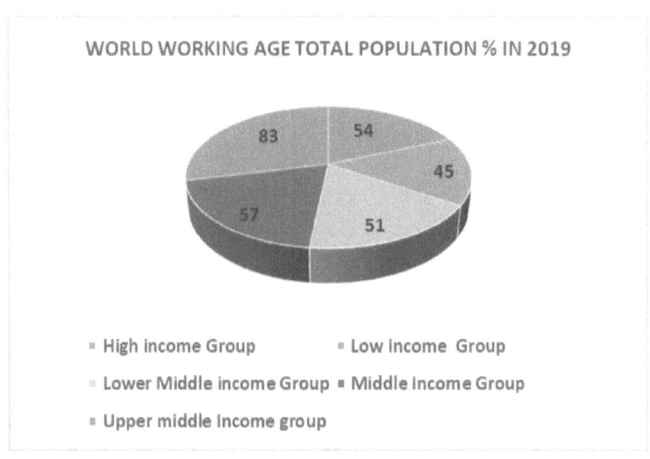

Chart 23b

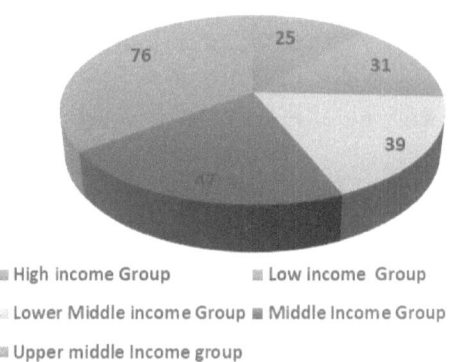

WORLD WORKING AGE YOUNG POPULATION % IN 2019

- High income Group
- Low income Group
- Lower Middle income Group
- Middle Income Group
- Upper middle Income group

It is known that in many cases, local unemployed people demand jobs in local organisations. But can we live with the demands of local unemployed people everywhere? No, we cannot. We cannot for a simple reason, and that is the nature of the designated work and proper experience to perform the job. Everyone has their specialty and interest in a work. But unemployment is at such a limit that we are failing to maintain our choice and specialty of work. In most cases, having a job to maintain a livelihood by any means is the target of unemployed people. When it is accepted, the production and quality are compromised. So it is rarely entertained. Generally, no employer wants to compromise the quality of the product, in fear of loss.

Coronavirus's attack on world countries has taken away millions of jobs through the mandatory closure of production and the hiatus of all types of production activities, including civil, structural, and architectural works in all countries, out of fear of contamination of the fatal coronavirus. It is an obvious and essential measure taken to preserve the lives of humans, but the pervasiveness of COVID-19 is very high. It has ruined the entire world's economic system in a really short time.

The extreme effect of the sudden closure and halting of all production activities and the closure of establishments and production houses has come as a bolt from the blue on the national workforce. Without a job, most of them have lost the roofs over their heads. Because of the closing of shops and hotels, they have lost food sources. They had lived on hand-to-mouth conditions with their daily or weekly wages, and then they lost their source of income, as they were not permanent employees of any establishment. Due to the sudden suspension of all types of transport, including rails and coaches, they failed to secure transportation and to find secure shelter.

When all the life supports were closed before the national workers, the only solution left for them was to get to their own houses, a long distance away, on foot. We have witnessed suffering of the frustrated, hungry, hopeless, and desperate workers on the road, below the sky. It's a disgrace to any country. The opportunities for their betterment were taken from them in all respects, and the corona pandemic was not helping at all.

POST-CORONA ECONOMY

The situation is not in favour of our society. The scarcity of national workers is inevitable in national activities and progress, due to the bitter experiences millions of national workers faced during the corona attack. We have to get out of this state of affairs.

We have learned from this horrible situation a very shocking lesson. We are very much lagging behind in management of emergency control to save the distressed workers. We failed to save the lives of many workers and failed to provide food and shelter to the desperate workers. Crores have been drained out, yielding very minimal benefit to the affected national workers. Positive efforts were given by different government, non-government, individual, and local bodies, but the exertions were not enough for the incident.

The bitter experience and agony of the national workers has seriously planted trauma on their family members. The painful deaths on the road and on railway tracks and the traumatic physical, mental, and financial suffering of the workers have raised alertness within them and their households. So a lot of national workers feel safe staying with their families, within a minimal financial budget. The position could be worse, and society may have to face severe moral degradation. That is a threat to the security and safety of the common masses.

The restoration of work is essential to bring life to the national economy. Security and safety of life should have to be provided to the national workers' group.

Their bad experiences might have to be wiped out, and a safety message should be apportioned to the workforce.

To strengthen our national economy like others, a new lifeline should be brought forth for this national workforce. They must be provided with a secure, tidy working environment. A national work distribution system with safety and security must be generated to provide a safe working atmosphere in the country for the workers.

Every national worker of each state, irrespective of sex, age, education, and religion, must be registered in a single national workers' job distribution and controlling system, and they must be issued a smart service card, linked to the same national health card. The smart service card will be used to register the worker's daily attendance. The digitally generated attendance will be the standard of wage remittance, sent directly to the worker's bank account by the workers' controlling board.

The establishments, organisations, production houses, institutions, etc.—whoever calls for daily or temporary workers should apply in advance to the local management of the national workers' board, according to their demand. The workers will be deputed as per the requirement of the organisations. The payment of the national workers will be credited immediately to the workers' accounts, as per the fixed wage rate for skilled and unskilled workers.

Service distribution: Any organisations, production houses, and anybody who needs daily or temporary workers should apply in advance to the board. An organisation in urgent need can engage the workers directly in an organisation, but they must register the attendance of the workers through the workers' smart service cards. That will automatically be registered and recorded in the service portal.

Wage distribution: As the workers' daily wages are fixed by the government, the organisations can send or deposit the total wage amount on the worker's ID to the worker's controlling board account for remittance to the worker. Or the organisation can pay the wage directly to the daily worker's account from their account, which is linked to the worker's controlling board.

The system will help control the daily service of every national worker in the country—their attendance, their position, and also their payment confirmation.

As the national workers will be controlled centrally, instantly we can get any record and data on the financial condition and health of a worker. The workers portal and ID card will be linked with the digitally controlled citizen health card. So, we can easily get and collect the information on any worker at any time. It will help to protect the workers at their distress. It will establish a worker's friendly work culture and strengthen national unity amongst all workers of any state. There will be no confrontation between regional and non-regional workers.

Housing, health, and training: There should be a *national workers' rest house*—in other words, *Jatiya Karmachari Aabas*—along with a *service assistance room*, with pure drinking water and a light and safe sanitation system for male and female workers. This should be constructed nearest the location of the business and industrial areas, controlled and supervised by a local government body.

Any national worker of any region of the country who holds the national workers' smart service card, linked with the national citizen health card digitally and centrally controlled by the government, can get a staying facility in these national workers' rest houses, with a very minimal daily staying charge and free health service at government health centres.

The government, NGOs, and other non-government training institutions and organisations, from time to time, will organise and provide free training programmes for the national workers in the service assistance room adjacent to the national workers' rest house, as skill development programmes. As the system will be worker-friendly and beneficial to workers, a happy atmosphere amongst the workers will be generated and welcomed.

The organisations and entrepreneurs who want workers for daily work or short-term work for any special programme may collect workers from the national workers' group and provide specific training to them at their training centres or in the training hall of the national workers' rest house. In this manner, we can easily fulfil local demand and obtain an experienced and trained workforce without any opposition.

The service assistance room will also be used by the government, NGOs, and other non-government health service groups and organisations from time to time, to organise free health-checking programmes for the national workers. In this way, every national worker of any state in the country will come under a single umbrella and be provided with a job, health services, and a staying facility, i.e. total security for the livelihood of national workers. It will, at the same time, build up a nationwide skilled workers pool to provide better production at all levels.

Every organisation and whoever will engage any worker on an urgent basis or by personal or direct contact without any prior intimation to the national workers' board must register the worker in its portal through the worker's smart card. The system will ensure a balanced work distribution to all and abolish salary discrimination of national workers. It will ensure the flow of trained and experienced workforce to get high-quality work and production that will boost national production and consumption, and strengthen the national economy.

CHAPTER TEN

WE ARE ALL UNITED

LET THE WORLD COUNTRIES COME IN ONE INTERNATIONAL TOURIST MAP WITH FRIENDSHIP

> Friendship is the only cement that will ever hold the world together.
> **Thomas Woodrow Wilson**

> Look at the sky. We are not alone. The whole universe is friendly to us and conspires only to give the best to those who dream and work.
> **A. P. J. Abdul Kalam**

A United World Spirit

Peace and Friendship

Communication facilities of the world are taking new forms as time goes by. From the age of stone inscription, we have now reached cell phones and the internet. The great universe is, at present, within our grasp. In a world of modern skill and applied scientific discipline, the world is a few seconds away. The vast world of a time past is now a small world with the expansion of technology.

The dimension of our life and thoughts has crossed our country's limit and has reached the doors of other world countries in many ways. Thus, we cannot exist inside our small territory and refuse or refute the reality of the social and cultural need to discover and distribute ourselves. Technology and skill have made our surroundings very small, so to achieve success, we require a greater boundary where the universe ceases.

Thus, we have to extend our hearts beyond our limitations. We have to admire the sayings of the Bible: 'Behold, how good and how pleasant it is for brothers to dwell together in unity.'

A peaceable, friendly coexistence of world countries can build a happy universe. The present age demands the exposure, expansion, and explosion of our cultures and values. Only good friendship influenced by love, affection, and a sense of responsibility towards mankind can do this. If we are not united, we cannot reach out our hands in hopes of friendly relationships. Basic and prime criteria never differ from nation to nation in the case of a standard of development and evolution. They just differ in process, technology, and resource availabilities due to natural and geographical restrictions. To gain self-reliance, countries need to look at the actual enemies of human society that are silently and in a disguised way destroying and preventing our society from making absolute progress. We have to discover the enemies and unitedly defeat them and wipe them out from society.

The enemies are not humans or machines; it is nature, the environment, and diseases that are silently poisoning the whole environment. The latest list, dated 20/08/2020, is given below.

Table No. 24

A FEW LATEST ENVIORNMENTAL AND MORTALITY RECORD THOSE ARE THE CHALLENGES BEFORE NATIONS, AND NEEDS SPECIAL ATTENTION FOR NATIONAL DEVELOPMENT.				
SUBJECT	EFFECTS	TIME	UOM	TOTAL
Forest	Loss	2019-2020	Hectaers	3323242
Soil	Erision	2019-2020	Hectaers	4473993
Toxic Chemical in Envoronment	Pollution	2019-2020	Tons	6258336
Under Nurished People	living	2019-2020	No	845352888
Water related disease	Death	2019-2020	No	538092
Mother during Birth	Death	2019-2020	No	197504
Children below 5 Year	Death	2019-2020	No	4856985
HIV/AIDS	Death	2019-2020	No	1074184
Cancer	Death	2019-2020	No	5247990
Maleria	Death	2019-2020	No	626778
Seasonal flu	Death	2019-2020	No	311984
Communicable disease	Death	2019-2020	No	8296228
Hunger	Death	20.08.2020	No	5753452

Table No. 25

COVID-19 DEATH TOLL:	CORONA CASE REPORT AS ON 20.08.2020			
Covid-19: GLOBAL RECORD	Case	20.08.2020	No	22847829
Covid-19: GLOBAL RECORD	Death	20.08.2020	No	796293
Covid-19: GLOBAL RECORD	Recovered	20.08.2020	No	15500291
Covid-19: USA	Case	20.08.2020	No	5745520
Covid-19: USA	Death	20.08.2020	No	177357
Covid-19: Brazil	Case	20.08.2020	No	3505097
Covid-19: Brazil	Death	20.08.2020	No	112423
Covid-19: India	Case	20.08.2020	No	2904329
Covid-19: India	Death	20.08.2020	No	54975
Covid-19: Russia	Case	20.08.2020	No	942106
Covid-19: Russia	Death	20.08.2020	No	16099
Covid-19: South Africa	Case	20.08.2020	No	599940
Covid-19: South Africa	Death	20.08.2020	No	12618

We see in Table 24 the latest data on morbidity and outcomes of various causes, and we see in Table 25 the latest record on the long march of COVID-19.

We will have a long fight to come out of the threats of adverse environmental effects on the human race, through the proper step of changing our behaviour, nature, and habits. We have to love our country and the nature and have to take necessary measure to preserve our natural wealth, like fuels, natural gas, coal, minerals, forests, rivers, etc., on which the human race is dependent. We have to find a way to get rid of death by viral diseases. The countries have to resolve the problem of scarcity of food for the poor and have to prevent death from hunger. Moreover, we have to win over the COVID-19 pandemic, which has frightened all world countries, including the superpowers of the world.

The world is struggling to discover the cure. Nations like the USA, UK, China, Israel, India, Italy, etc. have passed to a higher grade for the final application of the medicine against coronavirus. But all are waiting for the medicine. Our target should not be only the coronavirus. The aim should be to fight against all possible upcoming viruses. We cannot fight against a future problem in advance, but we have the chance to win over health problems by taking advanced health measures and building a healthy population from childhood.

Allow the world to come to a stage where we can say boldly, 'We are one. We are united.' We will gain the upper hand over our social and economic problems and come out as self-dependent nations. In such critical time of financial and health crisis due to Corona pandemic invasion, we the world nations should realise the importance of international friendship. This will benefit the global development in common national and international crisis like pollution, Global warming, preservation of water oil, and forests, education, health, unemployment, etc. But above all, the foremost target should be to build up a self-dependent nation by creating a zero-balance society in health, education, and employment.

Self-dependence is the first and most vital step to offering our hand in friendship to world nations. The countries need self-dependence through self-sufficient performance, establishing a powerful and successful economy and building a very healthy, wealthy, educated, and smart workforce.

POST-CORONA ECONOMY

Now the socio-economic culture and atmosphere demand a bold friendship amongst world countries. It is a challenging position for world leaders to wipe out all mental and political conflicts and barriers, and to build a secure, smooth, and healthy friendship that needs a peaceful environment.

COVID-19 has taught us that whilst we may be very powerful in the economy, arms, ammunition, etc., we are not sufficiently ready to give complete health protection to our citizens. The first demand of a nation is a healthy and peaceful life.

The deadliest pandemics are still unconquered from the prehistoric age. Pandemics never see rich or poor, powerful or weak; it never bothers with religion or territory. The most devastating encroachment of coronavirus has no boundary. The earth has to fight against global problems together. We unitedly have to struggle against the calamitous and destructive pollution in the air, water, and earth. We have to save the world from global warming. We have to fight with a strong hand against wastage in every aspect of our life and production world. Otherwise, we will be ruined by our reckless behaviour. We have to save our natural resources for a better future.

For the COVID-19 pandemic, as a safety measure, we have to maintain social distance, but to get rid of the pandemic in the present and future and to come out of mask culture, we need grand unity. Let us save our world unitedly. A global friendship can unitedly find out the solution to save our earth from all stormy weather. Only a collective effort can make up a flourishing and safe world. We have many things to do unitedly for the safety of one another. If we fail one, another will suffer.

We can collectively blow out the agonies and pathos of world citizens from the prolonged problems like unemployment, illiteracy, malnutrition, scarcity of food, global pollution, deforestation, pre-mature death, fatal and devastating pandemics, and so on. Those cause millions of deaths around the world every year.

Global issues are not manageable by a single country or a group of countries. Global problems call for global attention. The country calls for a vigilant standpoint to turn away from the barriers to national advancement.

The world has to fight against the problems unitedly. Pollution is the main cause of most diseases, deaths, pandemics, and global warming. We need to scientifically stop the root of air polluting agents like industrial ash and smoke, that countrymen inhale day and night. We have to make water and land pollution free. To provide a healthy environment to our men we have to take scientific measure to keep the river and pond and all source of water as well as agricultural land free from drain-water, wastes, and industrial chemicals. We take vegetables that, in many cases, grow in chemical waste–contaminated agricultural fields. All these increase the health hazards in the human physical structure.

The countries have to unitedly seek out a scientific solution. Industrial smoke from any organisation in world countries needs to be managed and be drawn downwards and be recycled for energy or be managed any other way to keep our sky and air pollution-free.

The drainage of industrial chemical-based waste water must be controlled and treated so that it cannot flow towards agricultural land or any water sources, to avoid water contamination. The waste water must be reprocessed to make it usable or must be drained into the proper drainage system after making it pollution-free so that it cannot defile human health.

We need to fight globally against wastage that claims the loss of more than one-third of our national products yearly. I have already noted in several chapters how we can attempt to save money through application of progressive projects on health, wastage, etc. Wastage of national resources must be minimised by global effort. Every citizen should voluntarily stop, misuse, and excessive use of the national resources to carry out national and global requirement. The scientific and administrative measure should be taken to save these valuable resources and save millions of dollars. By this way of savings of dollars from different sources every country can accumulate a fund to provide a job in every workable hand. That will in turn boost national consumption and production. Ultimately, the national economic system will grow, step by step.

Development and wastage cannot run together; the former is a blessing to a country, and the other is a curse to mankind. So wastage will never allow the rapid development of the state. We have to give great value to save in all ways and to stop wastage by all means.

Our nation can also save expenditure by remodelling the national child health policy and providing a systematic health assistance programme from the birth of a child. A completely controlled immunisation system can reduce the morbidity rate of children at an early age and of mothers. Only a complete health package can assure a healthy baby and a healthy mother, and can build a healthy nation. That will ultimately claim very minimal health and medical support in a total lifespan. Thus, the total annual medical expenditure could be reduced.

The state can limit journeys by private car by utilising it for minimal personal family use. To cut pollution from the discharge of carbon monoxides, nitrogen oxides, hydrocarbon, etc., we need to minimise transport on the road as much as possible by using carpools for officials. It will help reduce private cars and heavy-duty vehicles. In the mission of savings of natural fuel proper care and check-up of vehicles is required. Use of fuel-effective vehicle, use of clean and better fuel, use of electric and battery-operated car are the better alternative solution to stop unwanted pollution, save health, and save fuel.

POST-CORONA ECONOMY

All nations of the world have to save lives, save society, save nature, and overall save our world and humankind. We have to open education, spread health missions, spread jobs, and come forward to strengthen the national economy unitedly. We urgently need an explosion in research and development to save the nature from global warming and pollution scientifically, at the same time a global consciousness within us. We know and believe, that the great scientists of our world countries are able enough to do. It only requires human and administrative support of the countries with extreme priority. Let the consciousness come in practical sense of our mind actively in our daily life, not in only papers and sounds.

It's time to offer a hand in friendship to each other, make a healthy nation, and attain self-sufficiency, so that together we can solve global issues to keep our human society and establish world peace.

It is the time for global unity. It is the time of global friendship. It is better that we open our doors to grow our economy manyfold by sharing our knowledge, sharing our skills, and serving for the improvement of humanity. Let us open our national and natural beauty to our friends.

World countries have their own cultural activities, natural and national heritage places, architecture, religious places, and so on. Let all those be open to others. Share our cultural heritages to others. Enjoy the world's beauty. Open the door for others, to develop national tourism and earn money and ensure the happy breath of others with joy and merriment.

Let the world countries and their heritage sites be a traveller's destination. There are thousands of cultural and natural sites and architectural buildings and memorials scattered around countries worldwide. As per UNESCO, there are more than 1,121 heritage sites in 167 states. Out of those, there are 869 cultural heritage sites, 213 natural heritage sites, and 39 various mixed sites. Let the world's picture-perfect beauty, green nature, and silver streams be the peaceful, happy memories of our world travels. Allow the world heritage sites to be our centres of knowledge and entertainment, and sources of national income. Open the doors to the travelling interests of countries as a symbol of world peace and friendship. Let the world countries be a practical book of visual interest and source of knowledge on the cultural diversities of the human world.

REFERENCES

1	IQAir, 2019 World Air Quality Report (2019).
2	IRENA (International Renewable Agency), Renewable Power Generation Costs in 2018.
3	NRDC (Natural Resources Defense Council).
4	OECD (Organisation for Economic Co-operation and Development), National Accounts Data.
5	Our World in Data.
6	TheGlobalEconomy.com.
7	The International Monetary Fund.
8	The World Bank Data.
9	The World Bank Group, 'Social Infrastructure, Employment and Human Development', *Economic Survey 2019–2020*.
10	The World Bank Group, National Accounts Data.
11	UNDP (United Nations Development Program) Human Development Reports 2020, Multidimensional Poverty Index.
12	UNESCO Global Data (2019).
13	UNESCO Institute of Statistics (UIS).
14	UNICEF Global Data (2018).
15	Wikipedia.
16	World Health Organisation (WHO) Report (2020).
17	Worldometer.

www.ingramcontent.com/pod-product-compliance
Lightning Source LLC
Chambersburg PA
CBHW030937180526
45163CB00002B/605